P9-EMK-427

“GET READY TO SAY GOODBYE”

"GET READY TO SAY GOODBYE"

A Mother's Story of Senseless Violence, Tragedy, and Triumph

LaVonne McKee
and Ted Schwarz

NEW★
HORIZON
PRESS

*Far Hills,
New Jersey*

Requests for permission should be addressed to:
New Horizon Press
P.O. Box 669
Far Hills, NJ 07931

McKee, LaVonne, and Ted Schwarz.
"Get ready to say goodbye"

Library of Congress Catalog Card Number: 93-84523

ISBN: 0-88282-079-6
New Horizon Press

Manufactured in the U.S.A.

1998 1997 1996 1995 1994 / 5 4 3 2 1

AUTHORS' NOTE

These are the actual experiences of LaVonne McKee and her son Dwayne, and this book reflects their opinions of the past, present, and future. The personalities, events, actions, and conversations portrayed within the story have been reconstructed from their memories, also utilizing extensive interviews, research, court documents, letters, personal papers, press accounts, and the memories of participants.

In an effort to safeguard the privacy of certain individuals, the authors have changed their names and in other cases altered otherwise identifying characteristics and chronology. Events involving the characters happened as described; only minor details have been altered.

CONTENTS

“GET READY TO SAY GOODBYE”

Prologue

SUMMER'S END

There should have been music—ominous, dissonant music—played on the synthesizer to add a dark, discordant note.

There should have been a rain storm, water pummeling the sidewalk, frenzied people running along the streets, their makeshift head coverings of folded newspapers and magazines lashed by the wind.

There should have been distant thunder, the roaring sound getting louder as the sky continued to darken.

There should have been lightning flashes, the air charged with enough electricity to make their flesh tingle and the hairs of their arms stiffen in anticipation of impending destruction.

There should have been a monster, someone tall, powerful, so obviously deranged that mothers would race from their homes, grab their children, and carry them to safety.

Instead there were two boys, "best friends forever," walking home from junior high school, bright, joking, delighting in a day so warm and sun-filled it seemed to whisper of endless summer. Their world was one of street hockey and soccer, singing in the choir, Nintendo, pizza, and increasingly, girls. Their lives were suburban, "white bread," a throwback to the 1950s when Donna Reed and June Cleaver represented the ideals of American motherhood. They had both completed eighth grade—junior high in their community—and they were eager for new sensations.

For Dwayne McKee, this meant a future as a doctor or an architect. He was a skilled amateur artist looking forward to serious training where he could use his talent and intelligence.

For Jeff Townsend, this probably meant a future in business like his father, David, and older brothers who were involved in the alternative fuel industry. David Townsend was self-made, successful, and wanted his sons to follow his lead.

As they walked, Dwayne was thinking of the party the two boys were going to attend that night, the girls who would be present, and the kissing games they would play. He was also looking forward to sharing a pizza and seeing a video with Jeff before Jeff's parents took the two boys to the home of Shannon Panky, where the party was being held.

Dwayne was smiling and chattered happily as usual, but Jeff, now looking dark and secretive, was strangely silent. He appeared to have something else on his mind. Something seemed to be obsessing him.

If Dwayne noticed, he gave it barely a second thought; he was too immersed in his own romantic daydreams. The boys continued on to their first stop, Dwayne's family's large, white colonial-style home. Dwayne took out his key, but the front door wasn't locked, so they went right in. "First, let's get something to eat, then we'll shower and dress. I'm starved," Dwayne said, rubbing his stomach.

"You're always starved. You must have a tapeworm," Jeff retorted.

"Yeah, I guess so," Dwayne replied good-naturedly, smiling that radiant smile again.

Heading for the kitchen, both boys grabbed some milk and cookies. Then they went to Dwayne's room, where he showered and began dressing. "I can't believe we're graduating junior high next week," Dwayne said excitedly, buttoning his new white shirt and pulling on white slacks. Then he took out his favorite sweatshirt and draped it California-style on his shoulders. He turned to his friend. "Well, how do I look, okay?"

"You look good . . . as always," Jeff said quietly. "No wonder the girls like you better."

"Don't be silly. What's that supposed to mean?" Dwayne grimaced. "Nobody likes me better. I just make more of an effort, that's all."

Just then, Dwayne's older brother Brian, who had stopped by the house to give them a ride to the party, stuck his head in. "I'm the designated chauffeur to Jeff's house. You guys ready?"

"Sure. Let's go," Dwayne said.

Jeff nodded.

They headed out of the house. "We're taking my car," Brian said, leading the way.

On the drive, Dwayne chattered nonstop, but Jeff remained quiet. "You feeling alright?" Dwayne frowned and leaned toward his friend, his palm outstretched as if to feel Jeff's forehead. Jeff pushed him away and didn't answer.

"You sure nothing's wrong?" Dwayne asked a few minutes later.

"Nothing's wrong," Jeff responded.

Since Jeff's parents were at a neighbor's barbecue party, the boys ordered a pizza for dinner. "My brother will take us," Jeff said, and the two boys began watching the videotape Jeff had purchased. It was called *Faces of Death*. They believed it had been banned in several states, and having the chance to view it was as exciting as being given access to a magazine centerfold.

The video consisted of television news material, including images never shown on the air, as well as research films, scientific studies, and the like—all related to death. The tape showed a person jumping from a window and dying when striking the sidewalk. Another segment showed the free fall of a parachute jumper whose chute failed to open, the jumper splattering against the ground. There was an autopsy taped from start to finish, a man being eaten by alligators after falling into a pit, and other ghastly images. It was the type of video popular with fraternities when the members wanted to see who could prove their manhood by eating and drinking while being "grossed out." And Jeff and Dwayne both thought it was the height of "coolness" to watch the film eating pizza—to be visually grossed out while never admitting the images were making you sick.

Absorbed in watching the *Faces of Death* videotape, Dwayne murmured, "It must be fake," not admitting that parts were scary or nauseating.

The two boys began bantering back and forth, using adolescent humor to mask their uneasiness. Jeff's comments were at first similar to Dwayne's. Then they seemed to change. His attitude became cocky, defiant, mean. He began calling Dwayne names, mocking him.

Dwayne felt uneasy about the way Jeff was acting. There was nothing specific that warranted concern—he certainly wasn't being violent. It was an attitude. There was something about the time they spent together that was so uncomfortable, Dwayne seriously considered calling his parents to pick him up. He and Jeff could still both go to the party. They would just go in separate cars, easing the tension that had grown between them at the Townsend house.

Dwayne's parents would take him to the party.

But he hated to do that and make Jeff go alone.

Vacillating, Dwayne glanced at his watch. "Shouldn't we get moving? Shannon didn't want us to be late."

"*You* to be late, to be exact." Jeff was pouncing around the room like a panther, alighting first in one place then another as if he couldn't sit still more than a minute at a time.

"Jeff, what are you doing?" Dwayne asked with exasperation, making one last attempt to understand what was taking place before calling his parents to come get him.

"You don't need to know," Jeff snidely replied, adding to Dwayne's conviction that it was time to leave.

Suddenly, Jeff bounded upstairs, calling to Dwayne to follow. "Dwayne, come here. I want to show you something."

"I want to leave," Dwayne replied.

Jeff didn't argue with Dwayne's decision. Instead he said, "It will only take a second."

Jeff's room was upstairs, and Dwayne had frequently been there during happier times. This time, though, Jeff had gone to his parents' bedroom, and it was there that Dwayne was called. He entered, and as he did so, a hidden Jeff suddenly slammed the door shut, preventing other Townsend family members in the house from seeing what was about to happen.

Dwayne turned around and saw Jeff standing with his hand behind his back. Jeff had a big grin on his face. Suddenly he raised his hand and Dwayne was startled to see his friend holding a revolver. Jeff pushed the release for the cylinder and began removing the bullets. Frozen with terror, Dwayne stared at Jeff's grimly set face. Then he focused only on the gun, not the bullets. He knew that wherever the barrel was pointed was where the danger existed. Although he had never had much interest in target shooting or hunting, Dwayne had gone with his father enough to have learned gun safety. The primary lesson his father had taught him was that there is no such thing as an unloaded gun. A gun can always be fired, and safety comes from being certain it is never pointed towards anyone.

Dwayne gathered his thoughts, concentrating on his breathing and trying to act calmly. The lessons from his father came to mind, and with them the fear of what might happen if Jeff pulled the trigger.

Jeff placed a single bullet back in the cylinder, closed the cylinder and spun it. Dwayne saw Jeff look to see where the bullet had stopped. Jeff swiftly put the gun to his own head and pulled the trigger. The gun only clicked.

A long moment passed. Dwayne's heart raced. Then Jeff pointed the gun in Dwayne's face and giggled. "It's your time to die. Get ready to say goodbye."

"Jeff, put the gun down! *Put the gun down!*" Dwayne yelled.

Jeff said, "Goodbye," and pulled back the hammer. He didn't pull the trigger yet. It seemed to take a year for the bullet in that chamber to move.

But the barrel of the revolver was only two and a half feet from Dwayne. Dwayne knew that even if Jeff was nervous, he could not miss.

Dwayne focused on the barrel, staring at the bullet through the cylinder. It was in position to move to where it would be fired the moment the trigger was pulled. Then Dwayne shifted his gaze to Jeff, looking at his eyes. Suddenly he saw Jeff's eyes start to twitch the same way Dwayne's father's eyes tensed slightly before firing the shotgun during trap shooting. He had seen other recreational shooters as well, and all of them had the slight eye movement just before firing. Knowing there was no hope of stopping Jeff, Dwayne started to dive to the left just as Jeff's finger tightened on the trigger. Jeff kept the barrel pointed at Dwayne, moving the gun in the same direction as Dwayne's attempt to escape.

Suddenly the room exploded, but to Dwayne's relief, there

was no pain. He was convinced the bullet had missed him. His adrenaline was pumping rapidly. His head was aching. As he fell he threw himself to the side, his body jarred by what he was certain was his head striking the dresser.

A moment later a tingling sensation spread through his whole body. It was like a foot falling asleep—pins and needles—only it was through his entire body. It was as if he had hit his funny bone, but from the neck down. Then Dwayne turned his head slightly and blood began spurting from his neck. He looked up at his friend and realized that Jeff was laughing.

Time, having slowed, suddenly moved more rapidly. Sherry Williams had been in Jeff's brother Randy's bedroom when the gun was fired. She was the first person Dwayne saw rushing into the elder Townsend's bedroom.

Randy was right behind the girl and he grabbed the gun from Jeff. "What in the hell happened?" Randy yelled at his brother to call the emergency service and then Dwayne's parents.

But Dwayne was no longer focused on anyone else. He knew something was terribly wrong, and he was grateful that the girl came over, and wrapped a towel around his neck to stem the flow of blood.

Chapter I

"DWAYNE'S BEEN SHOT"

It was 6:45 P.M. when the telephone rang. The day had been a quiet one of taking care of business and helping the kids prepare for their dates that night. Mark was making service calls, and I had spent much of the day scheduling other calls for him to make over the next two weeks. Our daughter Kimberly, who was going on a date, had her clothing set out, and earlier I had laid out Dwayne's outfit for his graduation party.

Kimberly was doing her last-minute primping. A short while before, I had taken a break to go swimming in our pool before showering and putting on shorts and a blouse. Now I was preparing a light summer dinner for Mark, Kimberly, and myself. Mark and I would have a quiet evening alone together, a pleasant way to end the week.

It was Jeff's voice, and if the tone was not quite normal, there was nothing to alarm me until he said, "Dwayne's been shot."

"What?"

"Dwayne's been shot."

"Where?" I knew he was still at Jeff's house because it was too early for the party to begin.

"In the shoulder, I think," Jeff said, and that's when I began sobbing.

"Have the paramedics been called?" I shouted into the telephone.

"Yes," said Jeff.

"Are your parents home?"

"No."

"We'll be right there," I said, slamming the receiver onto the cradle, then racing to the bathrooms. Kimberly was in one, taking a shower in preparation for her date. Mark was in the other one. "Dwayne's been shot!" I shouted, my voice so loud that I realized I was becoming hysterical and that I had probably alerted the entire neighborhood.

I took a deep, trembling breath, but I could not get hold of myself. I was in shock. Neither Jeff's words nor my repeating of what he said made sense. Woodland Hills isn't a community where gangs run rampant, where drive-by shootings occur, where drug deals are consummated with bullets. *Dwayne had been shot?*

Mark and Kimberly came rushing from the bathrooms, buttoning their clothing on the run. I grabbed my purse and we raced to the car, not bothering to lock the house. An open door was an invitation to burglary, but all a burglar could steal was our possessions. Something had happened to one of our children, and a child is irreplaceable.

We drove the mile and a half to Jeff's place in three or four minutes. Police and paramedics were already there, their vehicles angled against the front of the house, neighbors gathered outside the Townsends' hillside home. We parked across the street and ran inside.

A melange of sights greeted us: the police, the living room filled with neighbors of the Townsends, Jeff sitting on a couch. Two or three policemen stood guard upstairs outside the bedroom doorway. We began racing up the steps. David Townsend was at the top. As we walked by, he said, "Don't worry, Mark. It's just a flesh wound."

One of the police officers stepped forward, "Don't go in there," he ordered.

"That's my son," I replied, my voice rising. "I'm going in," and I rushed past him. Mark and Kimberly followed.

Inside we saw our son Dwayne lying on the floor, a pool of blood under his head and neck. At least two pints of that precious life-giving fluid were soaking into the rug.

Paramedics had secured Dwayne on a backboard, with a neck brace keeping him immobilized for travel. An IV had been started, his vital signs were being monitored. I looked at the paramedics. Their worried faces belied David Townsend's comment. It was obvious they were not certain they could keep Dwayne alive. Our son was weak, in shock, with possible internal bleeding.

The reason for the IV was not to start fluids. They feared that Dwayne's veins would collapse because of the spinal cord destruction. They would need to be able to use emergency drugs to save his life. The IV would keep at least one vein from collapsing. That needle in his arm and the fluid that flowed from it might make the difference between whether he lived or died.

I bent over him. Dwayne's eyes were open. To my relief he looked at us and said, "Dad, I didn't touch the gun." His voice was barely a whisper. "I didn't do it," he repeated. "Dad, why did he do it? I told him not to point the gun at me, but he did it anyway and shot me."

I gasped, horrified at the idea that Jeff had shot him. It was an idea I had not previously considered. Dwayne seemed equally concerned about something else—what seemed to everyone else a minor matter. The neck wound and the bleeding, the concern about other damage, and the need to prepare the body for fluids, medication, monitoring, and anything else necessary meant that Dwayne had to be partially undressed. There was no time to consider anything except the fastest possible access to vital areas. As a result, the paramedics cut the legs of Dwayne's slacks rather than trying to slip them from his body. The few seconds saved could be the difference between living and dying, something that was not a concern to Dwayne. Most of his conscious moments were spent being horrified by the destruction of his favorite pants. The blood could have been washed out. A tear caused by his falling could have been repaired. But when the paramedics cut them, he knew it would be impossible to wear them to Shannon's party, to school, to the mall. Never mind the blood loss. The paramedics were destroying an essential part of junior-high coolness.

There was no time for reflection. One of the paramedics turned to me. "He doesn't have any feeling. We have to get him to the hospital quick."

Without wasting a minute they began to move Dwayne onto a gurney. One of the policemen by the doorway called to us, "Please wait downstairs." As if in a trance, I obeyed them, never taking my eyes off the doorway until Mark, Kimberly, and I were on the first floor. Most of the living room was a blur of people and sounds; nothing registered until I saw Jeff sitting on the couch, crying.

I still didn't know exactly what had happened. While I sensed that Dwayne was in danger of dying, I deliberately avoided dwelling on that thought when in the room with him. I told myself that it might not be serious, that he probably would be fine in a few days. Yet as I looked at Jeff, my first thought was that his tears were not those of remorse. They were tears of frustration. I felt that Jeff had wanted Dwayne gone from his life, and his pain was caused by the fact that our son was very much alive and that Jeff had been caught doing the shooting.

My anger rose as I stared at him. I was certain at that moment that Jeff Townsend had tried to murder my son. And in my heart, I knew that within a matter of minutes or hours, Jeff might find that he had succeeded, with the infection, blood loss, and body damage from the bullet. I was enraged, though fear and grief overwhelmed my anger at the moment.

I turned away. The wait for Dwayne to be brought down seemed interminable, going on and on and on until I thought I would scream. In reality it was only a few minutes until I saw the paramedics carrying Dwayne toward the front door, moving the gurney down the steps, out the door, and down the slanted drive of the house with us following. They ran a short way down the street to an intersection where, to our surprise, a Medi-Vac helicopter was waiting. Police cars, their lights flashing, had blocked off the intersection.

Mark, Kimberly, and I ran after the gurney, "Where are you taking him?" I shouted. We assumed it would be the children's hospital in Hollywood, never realizing that the distance was too great for Dwayne to survive. Instead, the men called back, "We're going to Northridge Medical Center."

We raced to our car and got in. Mark drove rapidly to the hospital. Northridge was only about eight miles away, but I was so frightened for my child that everything appeared to be taking place in slow motion. Those eight miles seemed to take forever. None of us spoke. The seriousness of the shooting was beginning to sink in. And one realization overrode the rest—this was not a simple shoulder wound as Jeff had first indicated; this was something a lot more severe. But what? Everything was suddenly so uncertain.

Chapter II

"THIS DOESN'T HAPPEN"

Northridge Medical Center's trauma team had been assembled within minutes of the paramedics reaching Dwayne. They were in direct contact by radio—the emergency medicine specialist, a general surgeon, specially trained nurses, and various technical experts skilled in X-ray, blood gases, respiratory therapy, and related skills—all prepared to share their knowledge until the patient arrived for hands-on work. The crews could also send EKG readings to a heart specialist, from the field, the ambulance, and the Medi-Vac helicopter. EKGs were used for heart attack victims, giving the paramedics the opportunity to perform procedures that previously would have had to wait for arrival at the hospital. And they could do them with the direct guidance of a top specialist.

The trauma team alerted the paramedics to the need for the IV access. Spinal cord damage often leads to spinal shock and the dilation of the vessels. The needle in the vein might become the only opening through which Dwayne could receive fluids.

The Trauma Room was a new concept for Northridge, which traditionally had utilized the standard Emergency Room for all procedures. It had opened in 1984, the staff originally expecting to have more heart attacks than any other type of patient problem. That was why the original monitoring plans called for field equipment related to the heart. Likewise, the room held what was called a crash cart, a special mobile cart filled with the various drugs and medical tools needed to save the life of someone having a heart attack.

In the first year of operation there had been six hundred cases treated in the Trauma Center, fifteen percent of them from gunshots and stabbings. Thus the staff was not unfamiliar with serious injuries like the one Dwayne had sustained, and they had been trained to handle both the spinal cord damage and the bullet wound. A few years later the percentage of violence wounds almost doubled—to twenty-six percent—because of gang violence. But children shooting, stabbing, and maiming other children would never be routine in Woodland Hills.

The trauma team needed information quickly. A portable X-ray machine was brought into the room to check Dwayne's spine. His skin temperature was taken, his motor skills and sensory abilities analyzed. A neurosurgeon was on call to close the wound. Everything had to be noted, including that which was not obvious. There was a chance that the shock waves from the bullet striking his flesh could cause more damage than could be seen immediately.

And Dwayne had to be kept immobilized. It was critical that no further damage be caused by the treatment.

◆ ◆ ◆

When we first arrived at the hospital, each of us reacted differently in order to get through the first traumatic moments. Kimberly rushed off to see Dwayne immediately while Mark and I were ushered into a small waiting area away from the normal traffic of the Emergency Room. Trauma cases are so serious that the staff tries to give the family additional privacy. There were chairs and a desk, and coffee was made available to us if we wanted it.

I sat numbly, thoughts whirling so ferociously through my mind that I was not really aware of all that was taking place around me. A social worker introduced herself, and from then on I was her pass in and out of the room. Yet what she was saying each time did not register. All I knew was that I wanted to see Dwayne, and I was convinced that no one would let me.

A nurse walked up to me. "Could you fill out some consent forms, Mrs. McKee? We need you to answer questions about Dwayne's medical history."

I nodded, forcing myself to confront the awful present. Despite my anguish dealing with the paperwork, the insurance forms and the questions about Dwayne's history kept me preoccupied for a while.

Meanwhile, Mark began telephoning the rest of the family to let them know what was happening. He called our daughter Deborah and her husband Dan, our son Brian and his wife Renee, all of whom lived nearby, and our daughter Carey, who was in Florida. Our daughter Gail and her husband were vacationing in Palm Springs, so instead of calling them, Mark called Gail's in-laws, thinking that there was no reason to disrupt the kids' vacation until more was known about Dwayne's condition.

A short time later, Deborah, Dan, Brian, and Renee arrived at the hospital and were ushered into the waiting room where Mark and I anxiously awaited some word of Dwayne's condition.

We all hugged, tears running down our cheeks. I was grateful to have more of my family there, but it did little to comfort me for more than a few moments. Then I was overcome with fear again. I kept thinking about Dwayne in the emergency room with the doctors, alone and frightened, and we couldn't even talk to him or find out how he was.

I continued writing until all the forms had been made out and the nurse got them, then I sat with my hands folded, gripping them in my lap. I tried to still them, to be calm, but I couldn't stop my body from trembling; my mind was whirling in turmoil.

Some time later I went to another room located just outside where Dwayne was being treated, and still in shock, I sat down. Mark went to a pay telephone to begin calling our other children. We were a close family. They had to know what was happening and would want to come to help.

When Kimberly came back from the Trauma Room she told me tearfully, "I saw Dwayne and spoke to him, though I don't think he'll remember me being there. I, on the other hand, will always remember." Her voice broke. "He said, 'Kimberly, I love you so much. If it really would make you happy, you have to marry Danny.'"

Danny was a young sailor, just a year or two older than Kimberly, and her first serious love. He was not well liked by Dwayne or us, though there was nothing really wrong with him. We just would have preferred another suitor.

"He was saying it like he was going to die," Kimberly softly said. "I love him. We always said, 'I love you' to each other, but I know this time he thought he was going to die."

◆ ◆ ◆

Nothing registered. There are some worries all parents share. The moment a child learns to walk, parents have to be alert to the possibility that he will run into the street when a car is coming. Then, he learns to look before crossing. When he grows big enough to have a bicycle, suddenly there are new worries. Dwayne, like other young children, was enough of a daredevil that we were never truly comfortable each time he went pedaling off with his friends.

Childhood is supposed to be like that. As hard as it is on parents, each new skill reflects a time of letting go, of trusting, of hoping that nothing permanent happens to this precious gift. You want to wrap your child in a protective cocoon. You also know that you can't. Your child has to learn to live in the real world, to risk pain in order to know joy, to risk failure in order to know success. And so Mark and I smiled and endured our inner fears each time Dwayne went off on his own, exploring his ever-widening world. He never knew how inwardly relieved we were each day when he returned home safely.

◆ ◆ ◆

These were the same feelings we had for all our children. Each of our children is uniquely loved. Each of our children is an equal concern. But Dwayne was the one in trouble now, and the nightmare we were facing was beyond understanding.

I still couldn't fully comprehend what had taken place. A gun? Our son Dwayne—shot? And by a friend? I experienced more than denial. I could not think, could not feel. I was overwhelmed by too many conflicting emotions.

The hospital had a routine for helping the families of trauma victims, yet that day, nothing worked quite as it should. Sally Wren, a social worker skilled in the field of trauma counseling, was immediately dispatched to help us. Twenty-four hours a day, either she or another social worker—or, during the third shift, a specially trained volunteer—worked with the family. The exact condition of the victim is given, though never a prognosis for recovery. Even when the staff thinks that the victim will live, they cannot make such a statement. Even under the best of circumstances infection may set in, a previously unnoticed heart condition may result in unexpected complications—so many things can happen.

Later—I don't know how late—I was desperate for information about Dwayne. Sally or one of the other social workers gave us regular progress reports, but in my hysteria, what they were saying did not register. I needed to see Dwayne, to touch him. I had to know he was alive. That was all that mattered, yet I could not believe anyone else. I had to see him for myself.

Trying to help us, Kimberly's boyfriend Danny, who had just arrived at the hospital to support her, slipped out of the room where we waited.

Hospital blues, the protective clothing worn by doctors and nurses when working, are readily accessible if you know where to look. Doctors have changing areas that are usually left unlocked. The physicians have lockers for storing valuables, but the room in which they change is usually accessible. There are stacks of blues in different sizes, and specific places for discarding worn clothing. Nothing is secured because there is no reason to do so.

Danny slipped into one of these rooms, changed into some blues, then walked into the treatment room as though he belonged there. This time Dwayne was awake, alert, and coherent. It was the first connection he could recall with someone close to the family. The earlier conversation had not stayed in his memory.

Danny touched his shoulder, they exchanged a few words, and then he left. For the first time, Dwayne seemed to relax slightly.

Instead of being grateful to Danny, I hated him at that moment. He had seen my son and I had not. How dare the staff let this stranger into Dwayne's room when I was denied access? I knew Danny was just trying to help. I knew he wanted to impress Kimberly with his courage and ingenuity. I knew he was doing nothing wrong. Still, I was Dwayne's mother. Mark was Dwayne's father. Why weren't we allowed in the room?

The fact was, Dwayne was undergoing tests, and had to be moved to different areas for the testing. No one could be present then. Only the professional staff involved could work with him. Anyone else would be dangerously in the way.

Danny had slipped in between tests. It was a moment of opportunity, and it might have been possible for us to do the same. But by the time we could ask, Dwayne was again being transported to another testing area.

When Sally came in she tried to explain all of this, but my emotions prevented me from hearing any of it or from understanding. Finally she left again.

As I sat there I was in denial, grasping at hopes. *Our son's young, strong, healthy,* I told myself. *Nothing's going to happen to him. It was a slight accident. The situation is rough right now, but he'll be home tomorrow. We'll spend the night and then go home together. Everything's going to be fine.*

Suddenly Sally came back into the room. Silently, she handed me a plastic bag. Taking it, I looked inside and gasped. It was filled with Dwayne's possessions—his shoes, his white pants stained with blood and cut with a scissors, his wallet, his watch. Only the sweatshirt was missing, and no one was certain what had happened to it.

Denial was no longer possible. I began to weep uncontrollably.

Hours passed.

Finally, after an eternity of drinking coffee and unsuccessful attempts at trying to support one another while we waited for word of Dwayne's condition, one of the doctors from the Trauma Center, a tall dark-haired man in his forties, came toward us. He spoke slowly and meticulously, explaining, "Dwayne has been shot with a .38-caliber pistol, the same deadly, powerful caliber used by the police. The bullet entered the right, front side of his neck and exited through his left shoulder. Although there are bullet fragments still embedded in his neck, I advise against surgery at this time because it is too dangerous to operate that close to Dwayne's spinal cord."

As I looked at him my heart sank. "A gunshot wound in the neck," I said, anguish in my voice. We all started to cry, letting out the pent-up emotions we had been holding back since I first got that call from Jeff.

The doctor was very professional, but hardly encouraging. He continued, "As yet Dwayne has no feelings—no sensation at all—from his shoulders down. We've stabilized him for now and we are transferring him to the Trauma Intensive Care Unit. Someone will let you know when you can see him."

He looked at me sympathetically. "I think it would be better if you went home and got some rest."

I hardly heard him. I kept thinking, *This happens to other people you read about in the newspapers. This doesn't happen to people like us.*

But it was happening to our family, and we had to look at the situation as calmly as possible to do what was best for Dwayne. It took all the self-control I had left inside me. I stared at the doctor, "There is no way I am going to leave this hospital—nor are Mark and Kimberly—until we know that Dwayne is going to be all right." We didn't know how long that would take, but we were prepared to move in if we had to.

Debbie and Dan went back to our house, cleaned up the dinner I had been preparing when Jeff called, locked up the house, and returned to the hospital. We were all so nervous. All we did was worry and drink more coffee, which of course only made me more shaky.

Time ticked by, each minute an agony, each hour an eternity.

I don't know how long Mark, Kimberly, and I sat there huddled together waiting for further news of Dwayne's condition. Finally, a plump gray-haired nurse with a kindly face came in. "You can go in to see Dwayne in the Trauma ICU. It's on the floor above us. I'll take you there."

My knees buckled. I could hardly stand I was so nervous, so frightened, but I knew I had to be strong for Dwayne.

We took the elevator up, slowly walked down a long corridor, passed through several sets of double doors until the three of us were actually inside the Trauma Intensive Care Unit. I looked around apprehensively. It was a long room with five beds along the wall and a central desk where a cluster of nurses were monitoring each patient individually. All the patients in that unit were in extremely grave condition. Their fate was literally a matter of life or death.

When I saw Dwayne, my heart practically stopped. "Oh my God," I murmured. He was strapped onto a "Roto-Bed" which was slowly moving him from side to side in order to keep his circulation flowing and his internal organs functioning properly. A cervical collar was fastened around his neck. His head was held rigidly in place by a steel brace attached to the Roto-Bed. IVs, tubes, and wires ran from various parts of his body. Just below the cervical collar the gunshot wound was visible. It had been left unbandaged to speed up the healing. Although I didn't want to see it, I had to and bent my head closer. The hole was about the size of a nickel. The exit wound—a long, jagged opening—was also unbandaged. I leaned against the bed for support and tried to hide my horror.

Dwayne looked weak, pathetic, and most of all helpless under all that equipment, but at least he was alive. He was awake and very apprehensive, and although he was in shock—or perhaps because of it—he was talking practically non-stop and didn't always make sense. "I remember the shooting and the helicopter ride, but

I don't know anything about my condition, Mom," he said, his words jumbling together. He took a hollow, rasping breath. "I can't understand why I can't feel anything." He looked at me and then, smiling warmly, added, "But I know I'll be all right." He was trying to be very brave. Still, he looked relieved at seeing the three of us at his bedside. He knew he could always count on his family for stability and support.

"I'm so terribly thirsty. Mom, can I have some water?"

I turned to a red-haired, thirtyish nurse with a pinched face standing nearby. "I'm sorry, he isn't allowed any liquids," she said. As time passed the nurses kept moistening his lips with a lemon-flavored swab, but it did little to quench his thirst. Every time a nurse came by, Dwayne begged her to let him have a bath or a shower. I think he thought that everything would be okay if he could just wash away all that had happened to him.

The rest of the family finally went home. There was nothing more they could do at the hospital. There was little rest for Mark, Kimberly, and me in the hours that followed. We were allowed to be with Dwayne each hour for five minutes, then taken back to the waiting room on the floor below where we talked, held each other, and tried to nap. As the night wore on, one or two of us at a time could go to see him, though never all three. There was little room for visitors. The patients required constant supervision and family members were in the way. No one was discourteous, but the nature of the work to be done was such that visits, even from the family, had to be limited.

At some point Kimberly went back to our house to bring me some slacks. I was wearing shorts when we got the telephone call and she thought I might be cold in the air conditioned hospital. But it wasn't the temperature that made me shake so violently. I was in shock. Any lying to myself that I did before I got Dwayne's clothing was over. This was real. Dwayne might not last the night.

I put my head on my knees, fighting for some semblance of control. I was hysterical, hyperventilating, unable to do anything but weep.

Mark held me, sharing the agony. He did not try to comfort me, nor I him. There was no way for us even to pretend that everything would be all right. Tears ran down his reddened face. We were close enough to share equally in the grief, yet that fact meant nothing at that moment. All we knew was fear, pain, and hopelessness.

Chapter III

A LONG NIGHT

Meanwhile, Jeffrey Townsend was being questioned at the police station. According to the official police report of the investigation, "OFCR [Officer] Hamilton interviewed SUBJ [subject] Townsend at the W. Valley Police Station. Present during the interview were OFCR Leite, SGT Tuggey and David Townsend (SUBJ's father)."

"OFCR Hamilton read SUBJ Townsend his rights as per L.A.P.D. Form 15.03.0. SUBJ Townsend stated that he understood his rights, 'Yes he wanted to waive his right to remain silent and yes he would talk to OFCR Hamilton without an attorney present.'"

The interview proceeded:

HAMILTON: Whose idea was it to go to the bedroom?

TOWNSEND: Dwayne said he heard my dad had a new gun. I

asked him if he wanted to see it. He said yes so we went upstairs.

HAMILTON: Where did you get the gun?

TOWNSEND: I took the gun out of Father's cabinet.

HAMILTON: What did you do with the gun?

TOWNSEND: I flipped the cylinder open.

HAMILTON: Was the gun loaded?

TOWNSEND: Yeah. Each chamber had a bullet in it.

HAMILTON: What did you do now?

TOWNSEND: I looked to see what made the cylinder move. I saw a pin. I closed the cylinder. All the bullets were still in the gun and the hammer was cocked.

HAMILTON: Had you cocked and uncocked the gun?

TOWNSEND: No. It only cocked once.

HAMILTON: Where were you in the room?

TOWNSEND: I was sitting on the floor in front of the closed bedroom door. Dwayne was sitting on the waterbed watching me.

HAMILTON: Then what happened?

TOWNSEND: I went to release the hammer. Pulled the trigger slightly to release the hammer. The hammer slipped from under my thumb and the gun went off. I was pointing the gun about a foot or less behind where Dwayne was sitting on the bed. At first I didn't see anything. Then I saw him fall to the ground. Before that I saw him duck because he thought the gun was pointed at him.

HAMILTON: What did you do then?

TOWNSEND: I dropped the gun. I went and got him a towel. Then I told Sherri Williams, my cousin, to call him an ambulance.

HAMILTON: What did you do with the gun?

TOWNSEND: I picked up the gun and put it back in the cabinet. I found the slug which was lying next to my parents' chest of drawers. I said to my brother's girlfriend, 'This must have gone right through him.' She said, 'Put it away.' I put it on the shelf next to the gun.

HAMILTON: Did you ever unload the gun?

TOWNSEND: No.

HAMILTON: Are you sure?

TOWNSEND: I had unloaded the gun before I checked the pin. Then I had reloaded it. I put all the bullets back. They had been on the floor.

HAMILTON: Your brother Randy said when he came into the room after Dwayne was shot that the gun was on the floor and there was a pile of bullets next to the gun. You told me earlier that you never unloaded the gun. Then you told me you unloaded the gun before the shooting occurred. Your brother says the bullets were out of the gun after the gun [*sic*]. Your statement and your brother's statement are in conflict.

TOWNSEND: Well, when the gun went off my finger was on the cylinder release and it opened up and two bullets fell out. I picked them up and put them back in the gun.

HAMILTON: Did Dwayne touch the gun before he was shot?

TOWNSEND: No, Dwayne never touched the gun.

Officer Hamilton also asked whether or not they were playing Russian roulette, and whether or not Dwayne said he wanted to play the deadly game. To all such questions, Jeff Townsend said, "No."

No charges were brought against Jeffrey Townsend at that point. Part of the reason was to establish all facts concerning what had taken place before filing any charges. The other part was to see if Dwayne McKee survived the night.

◆ ◆ ◆

At the hospital Dwayne was always awake when we went to see him. I suspected that he was afraid to go to sleep, that he knew he could die at any moment.

Just after midnight, it happened. In approximately thirty seconds, Dwayne's heartbeat—which had been fading rapidly—stopped. He lost consciousness, his body no longer able to function. There was still a brain wave, still the last vestiges of life as the trauma team worked frantically to jump start the muscle needed to keep the body functioning. Death would be a flat line of the brain wave. That would take two, three, or four minutes, longer if they were lucky. But if the heart stopped for much over a minute, the lack of oxygenated blood coursing through the brain would cause brain damage, even if the heartbeat was restored. Life could be saved if Dwayne did not become a "flat-liner." But that life could have all the quality of a vegetable if too much time elapsed. Drugs and a pair of defibrillation paddles used to electrically jolt the heart were brought to the table where only Dwayne's body continued to rest. Some other part of him—perhaps his mind, perhaps his soul—was no longer in the hospital. Dwayne was with his Uncle Bob, and Uncle Bob was dead.

The relationship between Dwayne and his Uncle Bob was not a particularly long or close one. Uncle Bob was Mark McKee's brother, and during the time the family lived in Arkansas, Dwayne spent some time with him. Though they hadn't been close, Dwayne felt comfortable around Bob. He gave Dwayne a sense of love.

Uncle Bob represented the broader McKee family. Dwayne never knew his grandparents. Of the surviving family members, Uncle Bob was the only one Dwayne came to know, and he died shortly after the McKees returned to California.

The seriously ill Bob McKee had been hospitalized during the last days of his life. His wife was by his bedside daily. One afternoon he realized he was going to die that night, and though his health had not grown obviously worse, he understood that he would never see her again. They said their goodbyes, then some time during the night, Bob McKee passed on in his sleep.

Approximately a year later, his nephew was fighting for his life in another hospital, in another state.

Dwayne had given little thought to his Uncle Bob, and none since being shot. Then Dwayne's heart stopped, and as he put it, "I saw the light.

"During the light, I saw my uncle. He was standing twenty feet away from me, and he was dark, kind of. The light was overwhelming, coming from above and behind Uncle Bob. His face was clear.

"When I was in Arkansas with my father, we went fishing on a boat. Uncle Bob gave me a fishing pole four or five years before I was shot, and it was my favorite pole. I treasured it so much that when I got stung by a bee and accidentally dropped it in the water, my father had to hold me in the boat to keep me from going after it. There were water moccasins and other deadly snakes out there, and no one could go safely in that water. I didn't care. I just wanted the pole that much.

"Uncle Bob knew that. There was this loving expression on his face when he gave me the fishing pole. And it was that same expression I saw when I looked at him during those thirty seconds when my heart was stopped.

"He put out his hand, and it was like his palm was straight out for me to stop. And he said, 'Stop. It's not your time to die.' He had a smile on his face, and I was comforted. It was probably the most comforting feeling I've had in my life. Ever since then I have felt like he's around me, watching.

"Gradually Uncle Bob seemed to be further and further away from me. I can't explain it. He didn't get smaller like someone off in the distance. His face stayed the same size. Yet we were growing farther and farther apart, and I couldn't tell if he was moving away from me or I was being pulled away from him. It was like one or both of us were on a treadmill being pulled back. Then Uncle Bob faded away and I became coherent.

"I guess my eyes were dilated. I saw a light. When I came to I saw it was the doctor with a flashlight trying to look into my eyes."

Chapter IV

AND EVEN LONG DAYS

At nine the next morning a graying spinal cord injury specialist found our family huddled together in the waiting room. "I've conferred with the other doctors and specialists. We've discussed Dwayne's case in great detail. Let me explain in the simplest way I can what has transpired. Dwayne has indeed suffered a massive spinal injury in vertebrae C5, C6, and C7, which generally amounts to permanent paralysis."

I gasped. "Of course," he went on, "this is not a final diagnosis. However, in terms of his future movement, the next hours will be critical," he said. "Dwayne will be constantly monitored for any feeling whatsoever below his neck—needles will be struck in various parts of his body to see if we can elicit any kind of reaction—and a close watch is being kept on his internal organs. So far he is breathing on his own, without the aid of a respirator, but," he paused and fastened his glance on a non-existent spot on the wall, "we're not certain how long that will last. All we can do is wait."

Again I cried. I never thought I was capable of experiencing such grief. I asked about Dwayne's future. Could he marry? Have children? Could he even continue his education?

I wanted to know about tomorrow, though I also wanted to be reassured. I wanted to cling to hope. I could not handle more reality if it meant life without hope.

The doctor seemed to recognize this. He said he did not have any answers. He could only say that, at this point, the situation did not look good.

As the doctor left, David Townsend, who had come to the hospital quietly, asked to speak with Mark. David was casually dressed in slacks and a sport shirt. He was prematurely gray, distinguished looking, and appeared concerned. Mistakenly, I thought he was concerned about our son.

David Townsend didn't ask about Dwayne's condition. He did not express sympathy or compassion. It was as though the fact that Dwayne was being treated in the hospital made everything all right for us. What could be done was being done. Now the problem was to handle the unknown, the charges that might face Jeff. It was suddenly Jeff who mattered, though Jeff was able to walk, to run, to pursue a normal life denied forever to our youngest child.

"I can help with all your medical bills," he stated. Then he paused and added, "I don't think my son should go to jail."

I stared at him in horror. David Townsend did not want us to sue him. To avoid that, he was willing to pay the cost of the care, approximately $100,000 in the short term because of the special equipment and intense attention Dwayne needed just to stay alive.

Mark was shocked by the callousness of the approach. Irate, he ordered Jeff's father to leave us alone.

Later that day there were other contacts. Our attorney was called concerning the case, again with a request that we not pursue the lawsuit. Mark was also paged to the hospital telephone, where a man identifying himself as an associate of David Townsend said that Jeff's family and friends did not want to see the boy go to jail. He said they would appreciate it if we did not testify against Jeff.

There were no threats. It was as though instead of a child being critically injured, there had been a minor traffic accident in a parking lot. The guilty driver was not insured but would be happy to pay for the damage to the other car out of pocket. No sense in making a big deal over a minor incident by a careless kid.

◆ ◆ ◆

Early on Sunday morning Patricia Klein, a reporter for the *Los Angeles Times*, arrived at the hospital requesting an interview. I didn't think about why she was there, and neither Mark nor I wanted to talk to the press. However, she waited to see us for several hours, never pressing the staff to get to us, never trying to sneak up to the TICU waiting area. Finally we felt sorry for what we were putting her through. We knew she was only trying to do her job, so we gave her an interview.

I did not think about why the newspapers were interested in the story at that time. Later, though, I realized that the shooting was unusual. Woodland Hills was simply not an area where children committed violence.

When the story ran I had another shock. At first, the police apparently thought that Dwayne and Jeff were playing a game of Russian roulette and that the shooting would serve as a warning to other parents to keep children away from hand guns.

> Los Angeles police have arrested a 13-year-old Canoga Park boy on suspicion of attempted murder for allegedly shooting a classmate in the neck during a game of Russian roulette Friday.
>
> The bullet severed the spinal cord of Dwayne McKee, 14, of Woodland Hills, who doctors said will be permanently paralyzed from the neck down, according to Lt. Bill Gaida.

The article quoted sources saying that during the interrogation, Jeff gave inconsistent statements about what happened. "Police said evidence contradicted the suspect's account of the shooting. 'It was physically not possible for a gun to have fired in the way he said,' Gaida said."

Ultimately the police lieutenant was quoted as saying, "I would say this case graphically illustrates the inherent danger of inexperienced individuals playing with guns."

The rest of that Sunday inched by. By Monday we were all exhausted. Mark had to get back to work. We ran a small major-appliance repair service, and there was just no way he could abandon our source of income now. He didn't want to leave me there alone, but he had to, at least for a short time to reschedule his repair calls.

Hour after hour I sat in the waiting room, visiting Dwayne as often as I was allowed. I still had hope, of course, and the determination of a mother praying for her child's survival, but I was spent, both physically and emotionally. And I was all alone.

As I sat there, eyes closed, I felt a tap on my shoulder. "Mrs. McKee?"

My eyes sprang open. "Yes," I said, my voice cracking. A thin man with watery blue eyes encased in rimless glasses leaned over me.

"I'm Michael Glenary, the neurosurgeon on your son's case."

"Is Dwayne any better?" I asked hoarsely.

He frowned and looked at his watch as if pressed for time. Then he began to speak. "The critical forty-eight hours have passed," he said as if I weren't aware of the fact. I nodded, not trusting my voice. He continued, "Dwayne still has not regained any sensation below his neck." I shuddered. "The bullet has apparently severed the spinal cord, and the damage is irreversible." He added without a trace of emotion in his voice, "Dwayne will be a quadriplegic for the rest of his life. He will be permanently paralyzed from the neck down." He stared at me for a long moment. "In my opinion it will be a medical miracle if he is able to even blink in his present condition."

The doctor walked away. I was alone in the hallway, stunned, not believing what I had heard, not believing that all hope was lost. I broke down and started to sob harder and harder until I became hysterical. I ran to the phone and called Mark, who came back to the hospital immediately. As soon as he came into the room where I waited, I ran to him and collapsed in his arms. "Why did we come back?" I asked. "How can this be happening to our family?" I murmured over and over again.

Chapter V

FATEFUL DECISIONS

Ironically, it was the children that brought Mark and I back to Woodland Hills, California—our children, the schools, the recreation, the food, and the combination of quiet streets and accepting neighbors.

In Arkansas the children had attended a small school with few options as to subjects. They lived too far from other children to form many solid friendships, and now that they were growing older, I worried about the lack of constructive social activities.

Rogers, Arkansas, where we had lived for more than four years, was a rural community where we had known financial success. We owned The Furniture Barn, where we sold new and used furniture and appliances. Mark serviced the equipment we sold.

There were only sixteen thousand people in the area, yet we had done well enough so that when we returned to California we could afford to buy the five-bedroom, three-bath home we now enjoyed in the Los Angeles suburban community where we had lived more modestly years before.

In Arkansas, both Mark and I missed the variety of restaurants we had known in California. I missed eating chicken liver from a Jewish deli. There were only two restaurants in Rogers—one failing in its claim to offer authentic Mexican food, the other called The Tale of the Trout, a seafood restaurant. The latter was the finest restaurant available if you did not want to travel one hundred miles to the nearest big city. You could dress up and make the night out a special occasion. Yet the menu never varied, and while Mark and I enjoyed fish, we sought more excitement from special dinners out. Ultimately, the trouble with Rogers was that the Ozark mountains and wilderness were a great place to visit, but our family craved bowling alleys, movie theaters, and the numerous other activities we had taken for granted when Mark and I originally thought we would like a break from the fast pace of Los Angeles County.

For us as parents, the return to Woodland Hills rather than a more Hollywood community was a compromise we made for the sake of the kids—fourteen-year-old Dwayne and eighteen-year-old Kimberly. The home we bought was approximately nine blocks to the Ventura Freeway, two blocks from George Ellery Hale Junior High, not much farther to El Camino High School, and within walking distance of a major shopping center. Yet our street was as quiet as a cul de sac in a wooded glade, an ideal compromise between the city living that excited us and the small country town we previously thought was a better place to raise the last of our children.

In Woodland Hills, you could look out over velvety green manicured lawns and freshly paved streets where sleeping dogs outnumbered passing cars. The children could play street hockey or roller skate without regard for traffic. Pick-up basketball games on the grounds of the junior high were common, and the kids rode their bikes to a private lake south of the community, where they could fish without the property owners caring.

Our neighbors were a mixed group of hard-working, successful people. There was a retired engineer in one of the homes, the high school coach and math teacher in another. A pianist whose career included playing for the philharmonic as well as being the on-stage accompanist for comedian George Burns owned a home there. And one family ran a mail-order flower business from their property. Even we chose to let our home do double duty, with me taking business calls for the large appliance service handled by Mark.

Compared with the movie-star mansions not far from Woodland Hills, the area was middle-class. But compared with the rest of the nation, the $300,000 to $450,000 homes were proof of the success of the occupants.

Mark and I were comfortable with the knowledge that the children could live a richer, fuller life than in the rustic, quiet, but dull Arkansas town. Yet what we did not know was that violence lurked amidst the tranquil streets and carefully tended gardens.

◆ ◆ ◆

It was pollution that caused David Townsend to move his family to Southern California. The smog problem, allegedly the worst in the United States, caused the state to become a leader in research into alternative fuel sources for the millions of cars clogging the freeways. Cleaner-burning and more efficient fuels were in great demand. Anyone with a product that seemed potentially of value was encouraged to establish a business there. Investment money was plentiful. Stock could readily be sold. That was why

Townsend, a chemical engineer and engineering consultant, went to California to form Anafuel Corporation of America, Incorporated, in November 1984. He wanted to profit from the fight to end the smog.

Anafuel's solution to one aspect of the pollution and energy problem was the creation of a gasoline blended with naphthas and alcohols. Townsend later explained that his company "bought naphtha at a discount price because it was less than the cost of gasoline, mixed alcohols with it, which was the cheapest form of raising the octane, and raised the octane to 92 and sold it as gasoline." The product was supposedly similar to gasohol in concept and miles-per-gallon. In addition, it was supposed to reduce the volume of unburned hydrocarbons and carbon monoxide.

Anafuel had a gasoline terminal, formerly called U.S.A. Petroleum, which was used for blending their fuel. However, its main office was the Townsend home in West Hills, California, very near where the McKees were living. The Townsends had rented the property from the time they first moved to the community in 1982 until they purchased it early in 1985. However, because they had not been able to establish credit, they bought the home in the name of their corporation. Soon the home was the corporate headquarters, with staff meetings, computer operations, and other activities all taking place in one or another room of the house. Rumors flew that David Townsend gradually began exploring the use of the corporate cover for other expenses as well. It was said that the business was paying for groceries, stockings, and numerous other personal items and that Townsend realized that he could use the business for personal gain, turning the corporate checkbook into a vehicle for helping his family prosper.

Many began to speculate that business expedience had turned to fraud. Hundreds of thousands of dollars in checks were coming into Anafuel from a variety of sources. There were patents applied for and won for the fuel process, despite problems with contamination of the gasoline ultimately created. The payroll grew to fourteen thousand dollars a week, yet plenty of money remained to be shifted away from the staff and investors. David's youngest son, Jeff, not quite thirteen years old, had a bank account so large that he carried his own automatic teller machine card.

Board members who may have personally questioned the excesses did not make a serious challenge to the improper business practices. The company seemed to be prospering despite the fact that the Townsends were said to be helping themselves to more money than David's salary should have allowed. The future appeared to be a good one for the company if the fuel could be sold in adequate quantity.

A couple of the board members, longtime friends of David Townsend, decided to give him a special present for his birthday on May 5, 1985. It was a .38-caliber revolver, a seemingly innocuous gift among men who enjoyed weapons, target shooting, and occasionally going hunting. No one ever expected that the gun would be the catalyst for violence.

◆ ◆ ◆

I was happy at first when the friendship between Dwayne and Jeff Townsend began. It's always rough being a new kid in a school where the other children have known each other since kindergarten or earlier. Jeff had also been displaced, his family having moved from Florida, so he knew what it was like to be a stranger in a new school.

On the first day of seventh grade, Jeff, apparently feeling a little lonely and uncomfortable, was sitting on the ledge of a classroom window, looking out at students passing by on their way to other classes. One of these was Dwayne, who mistakenly thought Jeff spoke to him as he passed.

"Excuse me?" said Dwayne.

"I didn't say anything," Jeff responded.

"You new here?"

"Yeah."

"So am I," said Dwayne, and the two sat down together, starting to talk.

The boys shared stories of the areas where they previously had lived. I later learned that Jeff claimed his family had been forced to leave Florida because David Townsend had bought his son a BB gun which Jeff had proceeded to use to shoot out the windows of an area motel. Whether or not the incident actually occurred, any adult would know it was not the kind of delinquent act that would cause a family to have to leave the state where they were living.

Dwayne also had a BB gun, something Mark purchased for him so that they could share one of Mark's hobbies. Mark liked to shoot skeet when he was younger. He owned shotguns, a deer rifle, and a .22 revolver. Mark enjoyed target shooting, and he was a firm believer in gun safety. He kept his guns securely locked away in one cabinet, and the ammunition securely locked in another cabinet. He taught our children to respect the danger involved with guns, to understand how to use them safely, and never to consider them a toy. He made Dwayne look upon that BB gun as being every bit as dangerous as a weapon whose bullets retained lethal power over a distance of a mile or more. However, when neither of the kids became interested in target shooting, Mark got away from the sport, simply keeping the guns locked safely away.

I like to think that Dwayne would have been troubled by hearing his friend brag about misusing a BB gun. Either he thought Jeff was exaggerating about whatever happened or he liked Jeff despite the incident. Whatever the case, they soon became the type of friends who would be at one or the other's home every day.

One afternoon when the boys were in Jeff's yard, Jeff brought out a pellet gun and proceeded to shoot a neighbor's cat as it walked along the fence between the yards. The cat was harmless, a household pet Jeff had frequently seen strolling through the area. Dwayne felt that the killing was meant both as a sick joke and to impress him with Jeff's cold-bloodedness. Instead, the incident troubled Dwayne, as would other acts of senseless violence. Yet such incidents were isolated enough that there seemed to be no pattern, and never again did Jeff kill an animal in Dwayne's presence. Still, it was as though Jeff liked to walk along the edge of what society considered proper behavior, crossing over only briefly, and then only to get a reaction from someone he wanted to impress.

Impressing people seemed important to Jeff. Dwayne was allowed to see bank checks Jeff's father had brought home from work. These were checks related to David Townsend's corporate activities. Altogether Jeff showed Dwayne several million dollars in checks that represented income to his father's business. The fact that the checks were left on the bedroom dresser rather than being immediately deposited into his account said as much about Jeff's father's ego as it did about the son. Each seemed to have a need for flash over substance. The elder Townsend was obviously successful in whatever career he pursued, yet his holding the checks for a few days before depositing them seemed a ploy to draw interest, and leaving them where they would be seen showed he wanted others to be impressed. The checks gave his son something to brag about.

The friendship between Jeff and Dwayne continued throughout most of junior high. Both boys were in choir together, and choir was one of the "in" activities for students at Hale, much like athletic teams in other schools. The students who participated in choir were an elite clique within the school. And it was this that enabled Dwayne and Jeff to be quickly accepted by other teens who might otherwise have excluded them because of their transfer status.

Jeff and Dwayne had another bond. They found that they took most of the same classes through eighth grade, a fact that always gave them something to talk about. No matter what other friends they made, no matter how different their personal lives away from school, the two boys had enough in common to always feel comfortable with each other.

However, as the months passed and we saw more of Jeff, we became less comfortable with him than we had been at first. There seemed to be an angry side to him, a personality that appeared more insecure than the usual adolescent "angst" experienced by all youth. We also noticed that Jeff seemed to have a need for Dwayne's company to the exclusion of others, while Dwayne was trying to broaden his friendships. Fortunately, Dwayne did not limit himself in order to keep Jeff's friendship, and it was obvious that some of Dwayne's other friends had no interest in the Townsend boy. We felt that their relationship was one that would probably diminish or end when they reached high school. As a result, we felt no cause for concern.

Of course, as adolescents will do, Dwayne and Jeff did get in trouble together occasionally. Even the most serious incident was one that could have happened to any curious kids. Hughes Junior High had been closed prior to the boys moving to the community and they wanted to know what the inside of the boarded-up building looked like. Together they broke inside. They explored the interior, then Jeff, pretending he was a swordsman, took a steel bar and slashed at one of the overhead light fixtures. Naturally, the action was worse than intended. The fixture broke, the glass shattered, and one of the shards struck Dwayne's leg.

Jeff appeared shaken by the incident. Using his socks as a makeshift tourniquet, he helped Dwayne stop the bleeding, then the two rode home on Jeff's moped. There was no long-term damage, and though we were angry with both boys, it was the kind of misadventure many teenage boys have.

In hindsight, it seems that there may have been one other motivation for Dwayne's friendship with Jeff Townsend. Dwayne was the classic "good boy." He was the product of a second marriage for both Mark and me. He was an intensely wanted child, like his older sister Kimberly.

Both Mark and I had mistaken "puppy love" for love when we were too young to be making mature commitments. Our first marriages occurred for all the wrong reasons, and we both got divorced when the reality of our errors became evident. By the time we met, we were more mature about life, cautious, and objective. I had four children by my previous husband, and I was in no hurry to rush into a second bad relationship just so the kids could have a man around the house. Mark and I made certain that we had mutual love and respect during a courtship that lasted three years before we committed to marriage.

Dwayne and Kimberly, the product of our second marriage, were raised in an environment where we were more involved as parents. We were older, had learned from our mistakes, and determined that our family life would be far more stable than it had been in our first marriages. We knew that Dwayne could not imagine doing anything that might earn our serious disapproval. Although the incident in the closed junior high school was wrong, Dwayne in his adolescent curiosity thought there was nothing improper about exploring what to him was an abandoned building. He might just as well have been seeing what was inside a cave in the woods.

Reflecting later on the boys' relationship, I suspected that just as opposite personality types are often drawn together in marriage, so Dwayne seemed to have been attracted by the hint of Jeff's dark side. There was a slight edge to the Townsend boy, a trace of danger lurking just below his surface control, like the tension that exists when someone raises a lion cub, wolf pup, or other wild pet. No matter how close you become to the animal, there is always the reality that one day it may turn on you. Although there may be no conscious thought given to the animal's potential danger, each time the growing creature seeks affection, there is the underlying fact that the beast may become wild. A playful romp may end with a vicious slash of a paw or a bite from the powerful jaw.

So it may have been with Jeff. There was a sense of rebellion against the norm with Jeff, not just the usual teenage testing of limits. What Dwayne failed to realize was that he could become a victim of Jeff's potential for violence, not just a shocked onlooker. And since Dwayne did not tell us about incidents that might have caused us to ask Dwayne to either end his friendship or be less involved with the Townsend boy, we felt we had no reason to worry.

◆ ◆ ◆

Most of that first year of friendship, the two kids, along with other boys and girls from the choir, did the normal activities of Woodland Hills youth. They involved themselves in pick-up sports, went to the movies, and played video games in the local arcade.

If there was a difference, it was that Jeff always had more money than the others. He bought music tapes, food, and anything else he wanted. He had that special bank account and ATM card. And in 1985, when he and Dwayne were in eighth grade, he spent seventy dollars on a necklace for a girl in school he liked. However, the girl was Dwayne's friend, not at all interested in Jeff, and unwilling to accept any gift from him, especially one so expensive. She returned it immediately.

The gift of the necklace was typical of Jeff. He tried to impress people with flash over substance. Jeff's father was making millions, and Jeff was going to be rich as a result. He could buy anything he wanted. Even his athletic interests were somewhat superficial. He lifted weights like some of the other boys, and he was involved with some of the pick-up games they all played. Yet he never really worked hard at anything. When he became interested in martial arts, instead of taking a course to train in the field, he bought weapons such as a throwing star—a knife-sharp device aerodynamically designed for accurately hurling at an enemy. Throwing stars are meant to cause incapacitating injury or death, and Jeff practiced hitting a tree with the weapons.

It was toward the end of eighth grade that Dwayne began to think that his friendship with Jeff would probably not continue as it had in the past. The two of them, along with their classmates, were changing. Puberty was moving through his junior high class like the rolling waves of water passing across a sandy beach during the rising tide. Girls whose friendship with the boys had once been based on their abilities on the baseball diamond or the soccer field suddenly had greater appeal off the field than on. The girls understood this as well. The games might still be a little rough and tumble, but when they were over, showers were no longer resisted, deodorant was applied, and make-up appeared on faces once devoid of lipstick and eye shadow.

Dwayne and his friends discovered the game "Truth or Dare," a variation of the game "Post Office" which had been enjoyed by all the kids' parents and grandparents during the same rites of puberty. "Truth or Dare" involved kissing as one of the penalties of a dare, and a growing number of his classmates hoped to suffer such a fate.

Not every one of Dwayne's friends was reaching sexual maturity at the same time, of course. Some still preferred biking to the mall for the video games instead of hanging around and watching the changing bodies of the opposite sex. But even the ones who still had stable hormones sensed that whatever mysterious forces had changed their friends would soon strike their own bodies.

Dwayne reached puberty early, as had Jeff. But though Dwayne was popular with girls as well as boys, he was not yet ready to date. He had no special girlfriend—many girls interested him, but not one in particular. And the girls liked him, liked the fact that he was less boisterous in the way he reacted to the new sensations of sensual desire. Dwayne did not make crude remarks or try to touch the girls without permission.

Unlike Dwayne, Jeff was a loner at heart. Although he seemed uncomfortable with most of the boys, he appeared to covet attention from girls. That was why he had purchased the necklace for one of them. That seemed to be why he was increasingly angry when a girl paid less attention to him or more attention to Dwayne than he wanted. He could handle the teasing of other boys, but he seemed to be outraged when there was even the hint of rejection from a girl.

Once when Dwayne was with Jeff, Jeff slapped a girl who did not respond as he desired during a conversation. The girl ran off crying, never reporting the incident to a teacher or the principal.

The failure to report the incident probably came from the fact that there were too many changes being experienced by all of them. They were riding the typical adolescent roller coaster of emotions, and none of them knew what was and was not "normal" in the way their friends were acting. As a result of Jeff's friendship with Dwayne, Jeff continued to be a part of the activities enjoyed by the choir clique who had hung together throughout junior high. Yet it was obvious to many of them that Jeff would probably gradually be eased out of the close social circle as they moved on to high school.

This was especially true of one girl who was Dwayne's friend. She had little interest in dating as yet, though she was keenly aware of the rite of passage they were experiencing. Graduation from junior high meant the entering of a more adult phase of life, a preparation for the time when she and her friends would be productive citizens, working at jobs, having children of their own. "Real life" was still several years away, yet she wanted to mark the specialness of their graduation by having a party for approximately twenty of their classmates. Both Dwayne and Jeff were invited.

"I was hoping I'd 'score,'" Dwayne said. He did not use the slang term in the manner of older teens. He was not ready for sexual intimacy, nor were such thoughts on his mind. He had eagerly looked at a copy of *Penthouse* magazine that one of his friends was able to obtain. He knew what it meant to be sexually aroused. But his fantasies, his desire to "score" that night, meant only that he hoped he could kiss one or more of the girls who would be present. A game of "Truth or Dare" would give him the opportunity, and he treasured the excitement of anticipation. He might not understand all the changes his body was experiencing, but they were far too pleasurable to want to return to the naïve years of childhood.

The party would be in the early evening. Dwayne was not certain whether Shannon's parents would be present, though it did not matter. None of them were interested in tasting alcoholic beverages. They had no interest in drugs, and would not have been certain how to obtain them even if they did want to experiment. And even the unfamiliar sex drives most of them were experiencing were not sensations they wished to fully explore.

Just as Jeff bragged about his ability to buy expensive jewelry, so did he like to offer his parents' services as chauffeur when the kids needed a ride. However, there were many times Dwayne was stranded with Jeff at the mall or somewhere similar when the Townsends did not pick them up as expected. He would have to call us for a ride, and thus we had all learned to be wary of his friend's "generosity." We tried to make certain either we or one of our older kids was available to pick them up whenever the two of them went somewhere that required a car to get home.

Thus, it was on June 7, 1985, an unusually hot early summer day, that Jeff again offered his parents' services for transportation, this time to Shannon's party. Not suspecting what horror the day would bring, Dwayne accepted the offer.

Chapter VI

FATEFUL REALITIES

On the sixth day after the shooting, Dwayne was transferred to the Rehabilitation Unit. We rejoiced that he would be in a relatively normal room, complete with roommate. The therapists would be working with him for several hours every day. Our hopes revived. He was on his way to recovery. Everything really was going to work out.

Dwayne had been an athlete, after all. He was physically coordinated and active as a child. His first word was the name of his favorite toy as an infant—*ball*. No way was he going to be paralyzed.

And then we saw Dwayne's roommate.

Joe was older than Dwayne by five or six years. He had been

in a traffic accident, and though his injury was slightly different from Dwayne's, the results were expected to be similar.

Joe was strapped into a wheelchair, one large Velcro strap around his chest, a second around his legs. He had what is called a halo, a metal cage-like device that is screwed into the skull and comes down onto the shoulders to keep the head erect. Joe also had a Velcro holder around his wrist so that a fork, knife, toothbrush, or other object could be placed there. He would have a plate of food in front of him, and he had to try to push, jab, or otherwise maneuver to get a piece of food on the utensil. Then he had to try and get the utensil to his mouth so he could eat. It was a task that, even after several weeks of training in rehab, was almost impossible for Joe. He had too little control.

Suddenly I realized the truth. "Dwayne is never going to move again," I whispered to Mark. The doctors were right. I looked at Joe and saw Dwayne in three months, three years, forever. . . .

Somehow Mark and I managed to reach the elevator without Dwayne's sensing our horror at the discovery. We held each other for support. The tears that fell from our faces immediately after leaving Dwayne's room turned into wracking sobs.

The whole truth had finally come to us. There was no question about what had taken place and what would not occur in the future. The mind of Dwayne McKee would be as quick and sharp as ever. Our son would continue to delight us in family conversation. But when it came to all bodily functions below the shoulders, Dwayne was likely to end up like Joe. And Joe looked like a bendable statue, the mind of a young man locked in a body that had to be endlessly manipulated into whatever position was desired.

Dwayne could fall in love, but he could never walk across the stage at his junior high graduation, much less high school, college, or anything else. When Jeff Townsend pulled the trigger on his father's handgun, Dwayne became like the victim in an old science fiction movie in which the mad scientist keeps a fully functioning head hooked up only to electronic and chemical equipment meant to sustain life. In the movies, the rest of the body does not exist. Our Dwayne still had all his parts. It was just that they were useless.

Chapter VII

SMALL HOPES

Dwayne's friends were telephoning him. We never learned whether the messages started before he could talk with them. In those first days we were too emotional to be aware of anything like that, even if the staff alerted us to the fact. However, when Dwayne was enough out of danger so that the nurse could hold the telephone to his ear, he proudly told us himself that one or another of his classmates had called, the strain of talking outweighed by the pleasure of hearing from others.

A few of the young people began to come to visit him. One boy rode the bus over an hour each way to visit Dwayne twice a week. For his friends, Dwayne's condition was frightening. The other problem they had was in discovering their own mortality. Children are immortal in their own minds at that age. They are invincible, destined to live forever without pain or serious injury. Only the elderly end up in wheelchairs. And death is something that happens to pets and grandparents.

Now they could see that Dwayne might die. No matter what, he would never walk again, never participate in soccer, wrestling, baseball, football, and swimming, sports for which he was known. If Dwayne could be hurt, so could they. If Dwayne's life could be taken from him. . . . Some parents brought their sons and daughters. Dwayne's Boy Scout leader came by, then offered to cut our grass so we would have one less concern. We appreciated the offer. To our delight, our lawn was mowed. In addition, sidewalks and stoops were swept—our neighbors simply added the care of the outside of our house to their chores when they handled their own. They did not ask. They did not expect gratitude. They knew we were hurting. They knew what our priorities had to be. And they did not want us to have to worry about anything more than absolutely necessary.

◆ ◆ ◆

Kimberly graduated from high school at 5:30 P.M. on June 19, the twelfth day that Dwayne was in the hospital. Debbie, one of our daughters, stayed with Dwayne so Mark and I could attend the ceremony with our other daughters, Gail and Carey. The girls used video cameras to record the graduation so Dwayne, Kimberly, and Debbie could see what took place.

After the graduation, Kimberly went out with her boyfriend and some of her classmates to celebrate. We picked up dinner, then returned to the hospital to tell Dwayne all about it.

Dwayne's graduation ceremony was held the following morning. He should have been singing in the choir, then afterwards, he, Mark, Kimberly, and I were going to fly to Florida. We had planned to spend eight days having a family visit with Carey—not having her race to California to see if her brother would live or die.

Kimberly and Gail went to the graduation. They wanted to be a presence for Dwayne, a way of both thanking the class for caring and to be there because the event meant so much to Dwayne. Again there were video cameras, but this time there was something more.

The choir wanted Dwayne to know how much they cared. No one was absolutely certain what had happened the night of the shooting. The news reports had remained unclear. Those who visited had heard Dwayne's story, and presumably one or more had had contact with Jeff or his family, but this was a time to reach out to Dwayne. They needed to show him that they cared. As a result, the choir, at the urging of two of the girls who knew Dwayne well, put together a cassette tape of songs that were special to him.

There was one more present for Dwayne. This one occurred during the ceremony, and it was a moment that brings tears to my eyes each time I watch it on the tape.

The moment had been planned carefully. One of the parents, not knowing that anyone from our family would attend, much less record the event, brought a video camera so Dwayne could vicariously share in the experience.

The choir rose from their seats, then started to sing as the parent with the video slowly panned across their young faces, which had been touched for the first time by the unpredictability of life. Many of the children were openly weeping, tears streaming down their cheeks as they struggled with the words to the song they had selected, a song that had never had such poignant meaning for them or for us. The song they sang was meant to convey to Dwayne the way his friends felt about him. The song was "You'll Never Walk Alone."

Chapter VIII

JEFF'S TRIAL

The police, who had continued questioning both Jeff and Dwayne, had become convinced not only that the shooting was Jeff's fault but that it was premeditated.

A short while later Jeff was arrested. Then a petition, the juvenile justice equivalent of an indictment, was filed for attempted murder and aggravated assault.

◆ ◆ ◆

Jeff's trial was approaching quickly. The evidence had been gathered at the scene. He had admitted to shooting Dwayne, though he claimed his actions were accidental. There was no reason for an extensive delay.

In order that there would be no question later, it was equally important to protect Jeff's rights. He was being held in custody at the Sylmar Juvenile Detention Center awaiting trial. The charges were too serious for the judge to let him be at home, circumstances that upset his mother, Marilyn Townsend.

"We didn't like our son being in Juvenile Hall," she said later. "They kept him for thirteen hours with his hands handcuffed behind his back. He was on a bench, and apparently the police took him back and forth to Juvenile Hall because the paperwork wasn't right. Finally, Sergeant Tuggey came in later that evening, and Jeff was still sitting there. His arms had fallen asleep at that time. And Sergeant Tuggey said he felt it was a terrible thing."

"He uncuffed Jeff and put him in the room, and they got someone there to take him to Juvenile Hall. He hadn't had anything to eat all day, and for a thirteen-year-old, I didn't think that was right."

Occasionally we would hear from one of the lawyers or the prosecutor concerning the case. We were told there were numerous stories being told about what happened that night, many of them in conflict. We thought that was good, that it would prove that Jeff and the Townsends were lying. We did not realize that, with no witnesses, assigning the degree of guilt would not be as obvious as we had convinced ourselves it would be.

Marilyn Townsend was the person who troubled us the most. She later commented that she thought, "It was just thirteen-year-old kids looking at a gun and who didn't know what to do with it, and it went off." She felt, "Guns do go off. You hear it all the time. Jeff was not a violent person. He wouldn't do anything. Dwayne and him were best friends."

Marilyn said that Jeff "didn't know what happened. He was putting the bullets back in. It went off and blew up, and a flash. He didn't know what happened."

"They wanted to see how the mechanism of the gun worked, and they couldn't do it with the bullets in there," she added. Then she said that Jeff told her, "He was trying to put the bullets back in, and realized that the hammer was still cocked, and was trying to get it back down; then it went off and he didn't know what happened—it just flew up in the air and Dwayne fell onto the floor, and it was mass confusion at that point."

Jeff had wavered frequently. The night of the shooting, his statement to the police included the statement "Dwayne never touched the gun." Later he claimed otherwise, saying, "When I took it [the revolver] out, he had reached for it and he grabbed it and I pulled it away from him."

Jeff also said of David Crockett, Anafuel's Executive Vice President in charge of Personnel, Administration, and Security, "when he bought the gun—he said something about a hair trigger, that it was easy to fire it off." Jeff claimed to have been present at the time of the conversation between Crockett and his father, David. He said that his understanding of the gun was "that it was easily fired. If you handle it wrong, it will fire off easily." However, Crockett later denied this allegation, saying of the gun: "If you cock it, if you pull the hammer all the way back to full cock, then it takes very little finger pressure to release the hammer to fire the gun. That's on most all revolvers. And as far as it having a hair trigger, that is a novice terminology. It was set for a certain trigger pull weight factor by the factory, and if it had been adjusted other than that, it was done after it was in the possession of David Townsend."

The ballistics tests conducted by the police lab did not reveal the handgun to have an unusually easy trigger pull. The gun was a new weapon, still in the box, requiring normal pressure to fire.

Part of the problem was caused by Dwayne, a fact that David Townsend would use against him. As Townsend later stated:

"The first story was—and it matched Jeff's story—was that they went upstairs to ask my older son, Randy Scott, who was in his room right next to our bedroom with the door open, when he was going to take them to the dance, because they weren't able to drive because they were both thirteen.

"He said, 'About fifteen minutes,' which gives them plenty of time.

"He thought at the time—and Dwayne testified at the time, too—that they were going to go to Jeff's room and look at some videos that Jeff had . . . or listen to some tapes that Jeff had."

"Instead, they went into our bedroom.

"The door was open. My son, Randy Scott, said he didn't know that they closed the door and went into our bedroom. He said it was a matter of fifteen or twenty seconds later—he said it couldn't have been very long—before he heard a loud bang and he thought it was a car backfiring. He still didn't assume it was happening in our bedroom."

Townsend continued, "According to Dwayne, they went in, and Dwayne sat on the edge of the bed and asked Jeff to see my new gun. I didn't even know that he knew that I had it.

"Jeff took it out of my cabinet. It was loaded at the time.

"He unloaded it and put the shells on the floor.

"They were both looking at the working mechanism of the gun. They had pushed the safety forward and opened the chamber, and while pushing the safety forward, they pulled the hammer back.

"Then after they looked at the gun awhile they were going to put it away. My son was crouched down on the floor, leaning against the door or six inches from the door.

"They put the shells back in the gun and closed the chamber.

"With the hammer back on a Smith & Wesson .38, if you close the chamber with the hammer back, the gun will go off.

"The gun went off and flew out of my son's hands and flew onto the floor."

Townsend explained that both Jeff and Dwayne gave the same story, though Dwayne later changed his version. David Townsend's statement was not totally correct, though it was true that

Dwayne did not accuse Jeff of trying to murder him that first night.

The police officers with whom we spoke, as well as people from the prosecutor's office, came to believe that Dwayne was telling the truth when he said that Jeff deliberately tried to murder him. That was why Jeff was charged with attempted murder and assault with a deadly weapon. That was why the prosecutor wanted to see Jeff in jail until he was twenty-one, generally the maximum sentence possible for a boy Jeff's age.

But Dwayne did not tell the truth that first night. He later confessed to Mark and me that for the first couple of days he just could not accept the reality of what had happened to him. He could not believe that a friend could try to kill him. He had experienced an event without logic, without reason.

Life was controlled to a thirteen-year-old. There were no surprises. Monsters and bogey men were easy to identify: Their faces were misshapen, they wore hockey masks, or they were otherwise identifiable as freaks. He understood death for others, but he was immortal, and the idea that his parents might die one day was an intellectual concept, not something he could emotionally grasp.

Yet suddenly his best friend was a monster whose appearance had not changed. Jeff Townsend's voice had not changed to the mechanical tone of a space alien. His face had not become covered with hair. His teeth had not been altered to a razor sharp series of fangs. No foul odor emitted from his body. He was just the same kid, the same best friend, he had always been.

Except that he wasn't. Jeff Townsend had a gun in his hand, and Jeff Townsend had decided that it was time for my son, Dwayne, to die.

In shock at the beginning, Dwayne was unable to admit the truth to himself or others. He had to think, to review the day over and over again in his mind. His memory had to act like a movie projector with an endless loop of film, replaying the same event until every detail became clear and indelibly etched in his mind. Only then could he admit the truth. Only then could he accept the reality that Jeff Townsend had deliberately tried to murder him.

But in some ways, this recognition came too late. By his being in denial the night of the shooting, Jeff's family, friends, and lawyers could argue that Dwayne's new statement was a lie. They could say that the truth was his statement when he was first shot. They could say that his comments after the fact were the result of anger over what had happened following the accident.

Nevermind Dwayne's condition when he was first questioned, the shock and pain he was enduring. The first time Dwayne gave a complete statement to the police was when he was in the Intensive Care Unit (ICU) the fourth day after the shooting. Detective Diaz came to talk with him. She tape-recorded his statement, and he tried to go into detail. Prior to that, most of his comments had been, "I don't know why. I don't know why. I just—don't worry about me. I don't know why." Early on he was barely coherent, but he was insistent that no one gave him any drugs. "I don't want to go to sleep," he said. I think he was afraid if he went to sleep after taking some of those drugs, he wouldn't wake up.

What mattered to us as well as to the prosecutor's office was that Dwayne was consistent in his statement from the time of the tape-recorded interview forward. Jeff, by contrast, frequently altered his story. Despite this the lawyers would be working from the statements made prior to the court date, as well as the statements made when each boy testified. There was a chance that the judge would not choose to trust one boy's account over that of another.

We did not realize what this could mean, of course. All we knew was that Dwayne would have to testify during Jeff's trial. Since Dwayne could not physically handle the travel between the hospital and the courtroom, it was decided to bring the judge, jury, and attorneys to the hospital to hear what he had to say.

◆ ◆ ◆

When the day came, a family waiting area would be converted into a courtroom. Tables and chairs would be arranged in a manner in which the judge could preside as he might in the courthouse. The court stenographer, security personnel, and others would also be present. Then Dwayne would be wheeled into the room in his bed. He could not be moved into a wheelchair. He was too sick, his body barely able to stand being propped.

We had been warned that the trial would not be easy in many ways. At the beginning, under the pressure of pain and shock, trying not to believe his friend could have shot him, Dwayne had protected Jeff. But when the reality sunk in, Dwayne changed his story. Jeff had changed his story many times during his interviews with law enforcement officers and others connected with the prosecution. Jeff was less credible, but both boys were young, barely into their teenaged years, and scared of what had happened, though for different reasons. The judge could believe that there was reasonable doubt. The judge could believe that the boys had been stupid enough to be playing Russian roulette. He could be sensitive to the fact that Jeff had never before been in trouble with the law, that he came from a "nice" family, from a good neighborhood. After all, white suburban kids simply didn't shoot each other.

There were other issues as well, though they would not be a part of the criminal proceedings against Jeff. The Townsends were highly negligent in many ways. Dwayne went to their home with the understanding that they, not Jeff's brother, would be taking the boys to the party. We did not know that the Townsends were actually going to a barbecue and were having one of their other sons drive Dwayne and Jeff. We did not know that a loaded revolver was available to any of their children any time they chose to pick it up. In our opinion, because Jeff was so young, his parents held great responsibility in what ultimately occurred.

◆ ◆ ◆

At about this time we separately filed a civil lawsuit against Jeff and his family. This was necessary to get critical financial aid.

Like so many self-employed people, we had insurance but were not part of an organization that could command special rates from the largest carriers. The couple that handled one of our policies found that such coverage was unprofitable and went out of the business. They did so without warning, and our catastrophic medical coverage was suddenly scheduled for cancellation well before Dwayne was shot. We had been told that the company was closing in March or April 1985, a warning meant to give policy holders time to find new coverage.

We were all healthy and unconcerned about such a situation. We found a good rate from Blue Cross, had our application approved, and sent them a check. However, there was a time delay from the paperwork and it was not in effect on June 7, the day of the shooting. For the first time in the twenty years we had been married, we were unprotected despite having done everything right to assure proper protection.

The hospital guided us through the procedure for receiving state aid, an experience we found humiliating. As small business owners, we were accustomed to taking care of ourselves, paying our own way, and delaying whatever we couldn't afford. We supplied our own benefits, paid all our taxes, met all our overhead. The only comforting aspect of all this was that the money we received from the state was considered a loan. The hospital bills would be paid, no matter how high they grew, and we would be expected to repay the government eventually. The taxpayers would not be deprived of the money spent on Dwayne. Yet even having to request that type of help was humiliating. What we were more shocked to discover was that if Dwayne recovered enough to go home, and if he could one day survive without several hours of special help each day, his medical bills over the next sixty to seventy years would still reach approximately three-and-a-half million dollars. It was a figure so staggering that we knew we had to obtain all the support for which Dwayne was eligible. And that meant acquiring any money appropriate from the insurance policy or policies held by the Townsends.

The money we sought from the Townsends was not meant for punishment. As the date of Jeff Townsend's trial approached, we did not want to see a financial package be a part of his penalty. We were convinced not only of his guilt but also that the circumstances occurred exactly as Dwayne had stated. This meant that Jeff Townsend was an extremely troubled young man in desperate need of counseling to prevent any other child or adult from being hurt. I wanted to see the judge sentence him to an institution where he could get help, where he could learn to control whatever impulses led to his shooting Dwayne.

I was not filled with compassion, however. I wanted Jeff Townsend locked away in that institution until the day Dwayne stood up from his chair and walked unassisted.

◆ ◆ ◆

As the criminal trial approached, we didn't know what was happening with the Townsends. Apparently the shooting brought out the worst in the family members' relationships with one another. We heard that David and Marilyn Townsend were openly and bitterly arguing with each other and that Jeff's brothers seemed to be living with great undirected anger.

The first couple of weeks in the hospital, Jeff's brothers were recognized coming by the hospital to check on Dwayne's condition. We never found out why they were there, though we suspected that they wanted to see if things were as bad as the reports they had heard. But we would have felt better about the presence of Jeff's brothers if they had left a message saying they had come by, that they were sorry, that they were concerned. So far as we know, they did none of that.

There were also crank telephone calls, the first beginning shortly after Dwayne was hospitalized. We had a feeling they were from the Townsends, though at first no one spoke clearly enough to be identified.

One evening, I had a call around 9:00 P.M. or 9:30 P.M. I went to answer it, but our daughter Kimberly said, "Well, let me pick up the extension in the bedroom. Let's see who it is, if they talk."

I said, "Okay," then answered the telephone.

The woman on the line—I felt it definitely was Marilyn Townsend's voice—said, "Is your son dead yet?" and then hung up.

I broke into tears. Kimberly came out of the bedroom hysterical, having listened on the extension.

"It was like listening to the witch from hell," Kimberly commented later.

Marilyn Townsend never confirmed or denied the calls. It was a shocking experience, especially with what we had experienced with David Townsend first calling Dwayne's gunshot wound "minor" and then his actions at the hospital. Assuming it was Marilyn who was calling us, it was as though she felt that we had caused Jeff's troubles. There was no indication that Dwayne had been the victim. There was no sense that they should have been responsible for supervising their children.

As time passed, we were never able to fully escape the efforts either to harass us or to refuse to accept responsibility. For example, Kimberly obtained a job working in a jewelry store in our local shopping mall. One day she was there when Jeff was no longer in custody. He came by, stopping in to see her. He seemed to have the same anger toward her we had heard in his mother's voice during the telephone call. She had to alert her manager, although Jeff left without incident. He had apparently accomplished his purpose, to upset her without doing anything to hurt her. He seemed to be vengeful, unable to accept the fact that Dwayne had been wronged, that Dwayne had been crippled, and that Dwayne was the victim of his actions.

It was as though no one in the Townsend family saw the shattered boy and the horribly changed lives of both Dwayne and his loved ones. Worse still was the possibility that no one in the family even cared.

On another night after the telephone call, Kimberly was driving home at midnight. She had a little blue Camaro she drove everywhere, and the car was familiar to those who knew us, including Jeff Townsend and his friends. She dropped off a girlfriend with whom she had been spending the evening, then drove toward a four-lane bridge over the freeway.

The road was a familiar one to locals. There were two lanes of traffic going in each direction, barriers on the side. It could be dangerous, especially if there was a breakdown, but it was relatively short in length, and despite the darkness, Kimberly felt safe.

Suddenly Kimberly was momentarily blinded by the bright lights reflected in her rearview mirror. She looked away, readjusting to the shadows of the road ahead.

Most drivers traveling on the semi-deserted road at night used their high beams. They almost always remembered to flick them to low when approaching another car coming from the opposite direction. However, when approaching from behind, they frequently forgot to dim them.

The car dropped back, then moved closer, coming almost against her bumper. For an instant she thought they would hit, then the car dropped back again. *Probably overtired,* Kimberly thought. *Or perhaps a little drunk.* He never bumped her, and that was a relief.

Just then the car picked up speed again, and once more it almost touched her bumper before dropping back. She was becoming concerned, though she did not worry until it happened a third time. Suddenly it was obvious that the driver was deliberately moving back and forth, never bumping her yet seemingly trying to make her think she was about to be hit.

Suddenly the other car picked up speed and pulled alongside her on her left. She could not see the driver, but the overhead road lights illuminated the face of the passenger. It was one of Jeff's brothers.

The driver turned the wheel sharply to the right, almost sending his car into the side of her Camaro. Kimberly was scared, yet she instinctively felt that the intention of the other driver was to scare her, not to crash against her car. He or she seemed to want her to panic, to turn the steering wheel sharply to the right so she would smash into the side of the bridge. Her fear turned to anger as she realized that she was the victim of a sick joke. She didn't know if the other driver wanted her to crash by over-reacting, or if the driver just wanted to upset her, to leave her shaking in fear or dissolved in tears. Determined not to become the second tragedy among our youngest children, she kept her car straight, accelerating when she felt she could see far enough ahead to not cause an accident herself.

The other driver pulled away, leaving Kimberly alone. She notified the police after returning home, though there was nothing that could be done. Kimberly could not identify the driver. It was evident that there was hostility between the Townsends and our family because of the shooting, so if Jeff's brother denied being in the car on the bridge, it would be her word against his. And most importantly, the driver had been careful to never hit her Camaro.

There were no paint scrapings to check, no physical evidence of what had taken place. The police believed her story, but a successful arrest and prosecution would have been impossible.

The police were sympathetic, but it would be our word against the Townsends', and since we both had reasons to be hostile, there would always be reasonable doubt about what had happened.

◆ ◆ ◆

By the time of the trial, all we wanted was justice, and in my bitterness I felt that the ultimate justice was for Jeff Townsend to receive an indeterminate sentence. I wanted him to go to jail and have to stay behind bars until Dwayne could walk again. That might be six weeks, six months, or a lifetime. It did not matter. I wanted Jeff to know that every day without freedom was a day when Dwayne was restricted to his bed or a wheelchair. He would still have more mobility than Dwayne. He would never share the physical pain that accompanies a quadriplegic throughout life. He would sit on a chair or lay in bed and never have to worry about sores forming, about festering infections that could further restrict his movements, destroy his health, or lead to death. Yet he would also never be able to forget what he had done to our son. That was what I wanted for Jeff Townsend.

Unfortunately, my emotions would not influence the judge. What mattered were the facts, and one of those facts was that Dwayne's testimony had to be taken from bed in the hospital. He had to be propped to testify, his body helpless. Jeff and his family would vividly see what the bullet had done. There could be no denial of the result, though the circumstances that caused it were in question. The defense story remained that the incident had been an accident. It had been a horrible accident to be sure, but Jeff never intended to hurt our son.

On the day the trial was scheduled to be moved to the hospital, Mark and I were present to help Dwayne through his testimony. We could not speak to or for him during that time, but we could provide moral support. We also would be able to physically help him if he began to spasm or his muscles tightened uncontrollably. Since he could not relax parts of his body himself, there were times when the tension was such that a doctor, nurse, or therapist had to help. Mark and I had learned how to do what were called pressure releases, and this would be another of our functions if necessary.

I wasn't certain how I felt about seeing Jeff again. I knew that I resented the idea of his being able to walk into the hospital when Dwayne would never walk again. The fact that he was being charged with attempted murder and that he might spend his remaining youth in a locked facility was not enough. I resented his freedom to enter the courtroom unassisted.

And then I saw him. Jeff's hands were positioned awkwardly, causing him to move with less assurance than when he and Dwayne used to play together. That was when I noticed the metal, the fact that he was locked into steel handcuffs.

Jeff had been brought to the hospital's makeshift courtroom in the same manner as all prisoners accused of violent crimes. He may have been a teenager—little more than a child in age—but he arrived like the most hardened of repeat offenders. His clothing was a detention center–issue orange jumpsuit. His hands were securely cuffed in front of him. Two large, well-trained, armed deputies—one on each side—escorted him from the van that transported him to the hospital. Only after he was in the hospital room used for the trial were his hands freed, though it was obvious that escape would be impossible. Jeff Townsend was mobile, but he was far from free. I have to admit that the sight was emotionally satisfying.

Dwayne testified for two days—Friday and Monday, the court

schedule at the hospital allowing him two days of rest in between. He was pale, the healthy tan he naturally gained from leading an active outdoor life having faded. He had lost weight despite the hospital's best efforts. His skin was stretched tight around his bones, his head lolled if it was not propped, and except for the lack of bloating in his stomach, he looked like the survivor of a famine.

My son was fourteen years old, not yet having started the final growth spurt that would take him into full physical manhood. He had reached puberty, but he was at that state in life when he was torn between the toys of childhood and chasing girls. He lacked the inner strength that comes from meeting the challenges of everyday life. He was a scared kid, hurt, sick, and exhausted. And now he had to testify.

I looked at Jeff and his family, finding them cold and unfeeling as they sat impassively through the hearing. I wanted to see some emotion from them, wanted them to accept responsibility for the horror their son had created because of their negligence. The only comfort was the orange jumpsuit, a reminder that Jeff was not free and hopefully would not be free at least for the rest of his childhood.

The young blond prosecutor was gentle, taking Dwayne through his story of what had occurred. She had him present the facts as he experienced them, emphasizing some areas where, we assumed, there had been a challenge by the defense during the earlier proceedings.

The defense attorney was not so gentle. His job was to pressure Dwayne into admitting either that Jeff was blameless, that the shooting had been an unavoidable accident, or that Dwayne was equally guilty. The defense attorney kept at Dwayne, trying to get him to say that the boys were playing a game of Russian roulette or that Dwayne's actions in grabbing for the gun caused the weapon to fire.

Yet Dwayne did not deviate from the facts he had provided to Detective Diaz. He told what he remembered, speaking clearly. His voice was odd to hear—high-pitched, more like a girl's—and he sometimes spoke haltingly because of exhaustion. But neither the damaged vocal chords that had temporarily altered his speaking voice nor the extreme fatigue were able to stop him. He answered all that was asked. He told the same story no matter how many different ways the defense lawyer tried to discredit him or catch him in a lie. He was honest about what had happened, honest about the early disbelief which had at first caused him to shield Jeff from the blame.

Dwayne's part in the trial would have been difficult for an adult to endure, much less a child. Due to the physical damage he sustained, getting through the ordeal required an almost superhuman effort. Yet Dwayne made it, and for the first time Mark and I realized that if sheer will power could affect his survival, our son just might triumph.

During the early part of his testimony, Dwayne's exhaustion was evident in his inability to fully control his facial muscles. One eye remained half closed, as though he lacked the energy to open it fully. His high-pitched voice was squeaky. And halfway through the questioning, Dwayne's muscles caused him problems. I had to wheel him into the hall and do a pressure release. I pushed his shoulders over and down, like an exaggerated variation of a shrug, in order to ease spinal pressure.

My heart broke as I thought of all Dwayne had to endure. Each day could bring a new crisis. Every moment of happiness had to be cherished, because he would never know when he might again be in trouble. And the situation was the result of Jeff Townsend's senseless violence.

◆ ◆ ◆

I turned to scrutinize Jeff more intently. He was doodling on a yellow pad provided for him to make notes. Watching his expressionless face I thought he seemed to lack any emotion about what was taking place. I felt that he had no sense of the enormity of what he had done. Certainly Jeff did not react to seeing Dwayne. He did not react to the fact that Dwayne had to be specially propped up in order to keep him from uncontrollably falling to the side and hurting himself.

I felt my anger rise, leaving a bitter taste in my mouth. I wanted Jeff to share the same private hell as Dwayne. I did not want him dead; I simply wanted him to know what it was like to go through every day of his life unable to have any more mobility than our son. I did not want to see him physically hurt. I wanted him locked away, his movements restricted by locked doors, barred windows, solid walls, and well-trained guards until my son Dwayne walked away from his wheelchair, his special bed, and all the contraptions he never should have required in order to live.

After two days of testifying, Dwayne's part in the ordeal was over. The rest of the trial was held in a regular courtroom. Mark and I could sit in and observe the proceedings, but that would mean leaving our son when he still needed us. We had to forego the experience of witnessing the testimony that would determine the fate of the boy who had shot Dwayne.

◆ ◆ ◆

Each day in the hospital was a day to endure, not to enjoy. Childhood is typically an adventure, filled with a combination of old friends and regular activities, as well as the exploration of the unknown. Before the shooting, Dwayne would have been playing with friends or riding his bicycle along streets and wooded pathways he had not previously seen. There were so many choices, so many opportunities, that the tiredness that would eventually overwhelm him was more enemy than friend. He did not want to rest, did not wish to stop enjoying the endless adventure that made up his life.

The hospital offered four walls, windows he could not look out without assistance, straps, braces, and protective restraints. Time passed slowly and rest was interrupted with necessary tests, therapy, and other procedures. Dwayne still felt that once he got home, once his world returned to normal, he would be walking within the year. What we did not realize was that though we are taught that rest advances natural healing, Dwayne's lack of mobility placed him in serious danger of dying.

Chapter IX

IN REHAB

The human body was never made for inactivity. The sophisticated systems that keep us alive and healthy require regular movement. Our ancestors were hunters-gatherers who roamed the countryside, finding wild fruit and vegetables, killing fish and animals that lived in the water and the fields. Even when they had permanent homes, their days were filled with activity.

As society became agricultural, the ceaseless work in the fields replaced the roaming of the land. Still, we moved forward.

Today we have a more sedentary society. We use computers and other equipment that keep us seated much of the day. Yet doctors recommend brisk walks or regular workouts, and many larger offices have special workout areas for their employees.

The alternative to activity is the slow destruction of the body through the failure of various systems, as well as the possible creation of blood clots. Anyone confined to be a bed for a long time requires special pads to reduce the risk of bed sores. Being limited to a wheelchair endangers the kidneys. And a quadriplegic has the extra risk of traveling blood clots that can cause a stroke or other life-threatening problems.

We knew none of this before Dwayne was shot, of course. And we were not prepared to think about it during the time when our focus was solely on whether he would live or die. However, after Dwayne was in rehab, there were regular meetings for the families and close friends of patients to teach them long-term care and the dangers the patient would face. It was all rather academic in my mind, something I had to know but which would not fully touch our lives. Dwayne was progressing. His attitude was generally good despite his resistance to the efforts of some of the support staff. The future would be difficult, but we felt that he was over the worst of the ordeal—until he felt the pain in his leg.

It was Friday and I was watching him in his room when Dwayne complained to me. "Mom, funny pains are shooting up and down my leg." I wasn't certain what it meant. I had heard of phantom leg pains that people experience after losing their leg through accidents or surgical amputation. They have feelings in locations where they once had their limb, though without the leg, such feelings should be impossible.

In my mind, if the leg pain was real, it was a hopeful sign. Perhaps it was the start of sensation returning. I reasoned perhaps the nerves where healing, the spinal cord somehow rebuilding the system that conveyed Dwayne's desires to his body.

Whatever the case, I knew the nursing staff had to be told of the pain. I went to the head nurse as soon as I helped Dwayne to the therapy room one floor above his room.

The head nurse did not seem frightened. "I'll pass the information on to the doctor," she said, her face expressionless. Dwayne's limbs were being exercised in physical therapy. During his time in occupational therapy he was trying to relearn how to make the type of movements babies make when learning to use their hands and feet. As yet, he had no sensation of most types of discomfort. Perhaps his muscles were just tired from the heavy use after the period when he was just laying in bed, healing from the worst of the gunshot trauma.

No one seemed overly concerned. After I went home Dwayne went to sleep. He was awakened around two in the morning for X-rays and some other tests. Although the hour seemed unusual, such awakenings would happen to him and other longer-term patients throughout his stay. The third shift of technicians had few outside demands on their time. Emergencies usually occurred at an earlier hour, and out-patient needs began around 7:00 or 8:00 A.M., running until 5:00 or 6:00 P.M. Although Dwayne would eventually be exhausted from being awakened at such odd hours, the timing made the most efficient use of staff and technical personnel.

I don't know what Dwayne was told about the results, if anything. However, I received a telephone call from the head nurse working with Dwayne early Saturday morning. Mark and Kimberly had both left for work. This time she sounded agitated. "You need to come to the hospital at once," she said. "The venogram, a type of X-ray Dwayne has been given, revealed an eight-inch blood clot in his left leg and several clots in his lungs. If not corrected, the best we can hope is that Dwayne will have a stroke. More likely he will die."

"I'll be right over," I said and hung up.

Trying to remain calm so I could do what was necessary, I checked Mark's schedule, then called the customer who would be the next person he was seeing on his route. "Could you tell Mark I will be at the hospital and have him call me as soon as possible?" Then once again I raced to the hospital.

Dwayne had an eight-inch clot in his leg and "several" clots in his lungs. I thought of the telephone call we believed had been from Marilyn Townsend. I thought of the paramedics fighting to stabilize Dwayne before putting him in the helicopter for transportation to the hospital. I thought of the large number of doctors and support personnel who had fought so hard to keep him alive after the shooting.

Dwayne could have died in those first hours—I would have understood that. A .38-caliber bullet through the neck is deadly. The pain of losing my child to Jeff Townsend's violence would have destroyed a part of my life. It would have been something that haunted me the rest of my days, an emptiness Mark and I would have to endure. Yet if Dwayne's premature death had to occur, then I could have handled that.

But now Dwayne was recovering. It was slow, of course. He could move nothing below his neck. Everything done for him required special bracing, hand feeding, the ministrations of others. Yet he was alive. Day by day he was stronger, less tired, more motivated. We had faced his death and he had survived.

After all that, I could not tolerate the idea of Dwayne's death being caused by a blood clot. "Please, dear God," I prayed. "Let him be all right."

Tears streamed down my face as I prayed over and over again.

I don't think I had ever known such anguish. This was not the time for Dwayne to die. I could not tolerate the idea that he had lived through such an ordeal only to have his body manufacture the cause of his death.

I parked the car and ran into the hospital. I was oblivious to everyone in the halls as I raced to his room. All I knew was that Dwayne might already be dead or dying.

Reaching Dwayne's room I paused outside, trying to get hold of myself. I resolved that Dwayne was not going to know how dangerous the situation might be. I would not let him see my grief and worry. If he died, it would be in comfort, not in the midst of watching his mother's anguish. I wiped away my tears, fixed my makeup, and forced a smile on my face. I practiced my words as tears choked me and walked in. "Hi, Dwayne. Just happened by to see how you're doing. Gee, you're looking good. You'll be out of that bed and walking in no time."

Dwayne lay in bed, an IV in his arm. He had not needed an IV since those first days after being shot. At that point, they had to keep his veins open to be certain critical body functions did not stop. But the IVs had stopped. Dwayne had been making it on his own.

Staring at the IV, I felt it meant the beginning of the end. What had not happened that terrible night in June was apparently fated to occur. I was losing Dwayne. He looked up at me and smiled. I thought he was trying to be so brave. The reality was more likely that he had no idea how serious his condition had become. He was only fourteen years old, an age when medical care or life-threatening illnesses are difficult to comprehend. His happiness was that of someone naïve, not someone trying to put on a false front as I was doing.

The nurse came into the room. "Would you leave for a few moments," she said. "I need to take care of something for Dwayne." I forced yet another smile, then went out into the hall as she closed the door behind me to give him privacy. As soon as I knew he could not see me, I leaned against the wall and started to weep uncontrollably.

Sally the social worker came by as I was crying. We talked, and I shared my fears. There was nothing she could say, nothing she could do. Talking helped me gain enough control to go to the telephone and try to reach Mark and Kimberly. They both came to the hospital immediately.

As we stood outside Dwayne's room, Dr. Sherman, a pulmonary specialist who had been involved with Dwayne's case walked up. He explained, "The IVs are to allow the use of an anti-coagulating agent. For the next week, we'll try to thin the blood clots. There are several techniques that might work, and we plan to use them all. We'll monitor Dwayne very carefully, and if all goes well he'll remain on one form or another of the anti-clotting drugs for the next year."

Again we were forced to understand the true impact of the bullet that had penetrated Dwayne's spinal cord. As a body fails to be used in a normal manner, it begins to destroy itself. Bed sores, for example, are not simple skin problems such as acne or the blisters you get when working in a garden without wearing gloves. They are festering wounds that can penetrate to the bone, creating infection so serious that prior to the discovery of antibiotics, they were a major cause of death for the paralyzed and infirm who experienced them.

People in wheelchairs often lean at an odd angle due to their inability to sit fully erect. There can also be curvature of the spine. All of these frequently lead to kidney damage. Dwayne had one kidney smaller than the other. Some victims find that one of their kidneys fails to function and has to be removed.

During the next several years, our son could do everything right and still face the life-threatening failure of part of his body. He would never know a moment free from the potential of destructive illness. Each day could bring a new crisis. Every moment of happiness was to be cherished, because he would never know when he might again be in grave trouble. And the situation was the result of Jeff Townsend's senseless violence.

When I had rushed to Dwayne's side because of the newly discovered blood clots, I realized that Jeff's threat to our son's life did not end when the trigger was pulled. Jeff's actions, whether accidental or deliberate, would continue to threaten Dwayne day after day and year after year. No matter how many skills he regained, the risk of blood clots, infections, and similar problems would remain with him the rest of his life. Once again I prayed that Jeff Townsend would pay for what he had done to our son.

◆ ◆ ◆

Shortly thereafter the trial ended. The police officers told us that they were convinced that Jeff had attempted to murder our son. The prosecutor's office believed the same thing. There had been too many conflicting stories coming from Jeff. Everyone believed Dwayne—everyone except the judge, who could not reach a positive conclusion. He felt that there was just enough reasonable doubt that he had to find Jeff guilty only of violence caused by negligence, not carefully planned assault with intent to kill.

When I heard the verdict, I knew that no one would really be held responsible for Dwayne's shooting. Jeff had been negligent, not criminal, and the extent of his punishment was a year of his life disrupted by appointments with a therapist and a probation officer. David Townsend had been negligent, not criminal, and his life had been troubled only to the extent of having to pay for his son's legal and counseling fees. Marilyn Townsend had been negligent, not criminal, and her life had been troubled only by embarrassment.

Jeff had never been in trouble before spending several weeks in the juvenile detention center. He would serve no more time in jail or in a psychiatric treatment facility. He was sentenced to a year's probation, the greatest restriction being the necessity of reporting to a parole officer and occasionally seeing a therapist during the next twelve months.

Admittedly, though many others shared our anger concerning what had been done to Dwayne, some involved with the case—for instance, the judge and defense attorneys—believed that the shooting was accidental. They thought Jeff could have been playing a deadly game. He did not mean to kill or cripple Dwayne, but to scare him with the loaded revolver. They felt that he may even have meant to pull the trigger, never realizing that the bullet would hit Dwayne.

Nancy Lidamore, the prosecutor, was troubled by the unique nature of the case. "These were two kids who were seemingly very good kids from normal families. The suspect, Jeff, seemed to come from a normal, caring family. Both were affluent, not typical of the kids who go through the justice system. They were best friends who liked and trusted each other. I never could understand why it happened."

The prosecutor explained that her firearms expert carefully analyzed the statement Jeff made about the shooting, comparing it with what was possible with the revolver. The expert found that Jeff's story was impossible. There was no way the incident could have taken place as Jeff explained it. That was why she pressed for attempted murder.

The Townsends hired their own expert. He was a former high-ranking officer in the Los Angeles Police Department who had extensively investigated shootings during his last years on the force. However, he was neither a firearms expert nor a forensics expert as was the prosecution's witness. He lacked the technical knowledge to have his testimony considered credible. There was no question that Jeff had acted quite differently than his statement indicated.

The prosecutor said, "The physical evidence was consistent with the shooting not being an accident."

Despite this, the case was troubling to Nancy Lidamore. The boys were extraordinarily young. Thirteen- and fourteen-year-olds normally do not shoot, maim, or kill each other. After two years in private practice and ten years with the prosecutor's office, she could only recall one other such case, and that involved a twelve-year-old murderer. Yet her work involved her with cases in some of Los Angeles's most active gang locations.

"It was a very sad case. There was no reason for the shooting. These were best friends, not strangers." Yet there was no question of Jeff's guilt. "There has never been an answer in my mind as to why it happened," she added.

Ultimately Jeff, like other juveniles, was protected from his own actions. He had faced what was called a "petition." When he was found guilty, the court referred to the action as a "sustained petition," the equivalent of a conviction for an adult. The case was a felony and the penalty was decided within those parameters. However, by calling it a "sustained petition," when Jeff reached adulthood and either wanted to go into a highly trained profession such as law or medicine, or went looking for a job, he could honestly say he had never been convicted of a felony. As Nancy Lidamore explained the reasoning, there are many kids who commit serious crimes such as car theft, while juveniles, who manage to get straightened out in the system. They go on to become honest, productive citizens as adults. There is no reason to stigmatize their last fifty or more years for something they did in their first ten or twenty.

But for those of us who suffered the horrible results, it was a bitter pill to swallow. Though Jeff was guilty of a felony, the court record indicated only that a petition was sustained. There would be no record of a felony arrest or conviction as there would have been with an adult.

Had the Townsends been at home to take the boys to the party, as we expected, there would have been adequate supervision to prevent Jeff from obtaining the revolver. Instead, they were negligent by leaving without letting us know. It was true that one of their sons agreed to take the boys, and there was nothing wrong with that. But we knew none of this in advance, and might have preferred to take the boys ourselves. Certainly, what happened showed that their judgment was not what it should have been. We were the victims of severe negligence on the part of the parents, from their leaving a loaded gun where a child could get it to not supervising Jeff and Dwayne as we expected.

Perhaps the anger and bitterness would have been less had

there been any compassion on their part. Perhaps my rage could have been tempered had anyone even once said they were sorry for Dwayne, or expressed concern for my son, who would spend his life in a wheelchair because of the shooting.

Chapter X

DAVID TOWNSEND

David Townsend's business was in trouble. His son's actions had generated a lot of adverse publicity. He was already having trouble creating a salable product. According to David Crockett, the fuel additive should have worked, but inadequate attention was paid to quality control. The final gasoline mixture was contaminated; it could not be successfully sold. Money had been available for the start-up company, and the patented process seemed to have passed laboratory testing. Once the fuel was mixed, however, the contamination prevented sales. Cash flow was almost non-existent, and new investors could not be obtained because of the publicity from the shooting. David Townsend had been in a precarious enough position when he could devote all his time to selling and easing the concerns of those who worried about when the business would start generating any money. Now the time he had to take to handle his son's legal problems was like a high wind striking a house of cards.

There was also grumbling among Townsend's corporate board of directors, who felt the Townsends were buying cars, paying for personal insurance, and purchasing food and other items with corporate money. They mentioned this to Townsend, but David was president, chief executive officer, chairman of the board, holder of the patent—basically, the company. He could fire anyone who made too strong a criticism, and while opposition had not been strong before the shooting, he knew problems might increase afterwards.

"I even signed for two brand-new Buicks in California, again, using my [personal] credit rating," said Crockett. "One car for him [Townsend] as president of the corporation, one car to his daughter-in-law, Sandy, as courier, to go back and forth from L.A. to Ojai. They never paid for them [*sic*] cars. That car company is still looking for me."

Crockett explained that while the cars were intended to be used for Anafuel business, they were used more extensively on a personal basis. Then Townsend traded one of the Buicks for a Cadillac, which was then sought in Orange County for repossession. David Townsend brought the Cadillac to Canoga Park in Los Angeles, but according to Crockett, "the repossession company ended up getting them all eventually." Since Crockett had guaranteed the loan and was financially responsible for the results of Townsend's machinations, it was his credit rating that was destroyed.

"Everything it looked like was being done for the company, Townsend was doing for himself, only to his personal benefit, in the name of the company."

The Townsends also knew that after the shooting there might

be serious personal financial problems for them. When the arrest came, Jeff was given a petition which stated he was charged with attempted murder and assault with a deadly weapon. Because he was a juvenile with no prior record, the sustained petition involved a lesser charge. However, when the petition was sustained Jeff was, in fact, found guilty of aggravated assault. That meant there would be some degree of financial liability on the part of the Townsends.

Jeff's parents apparently realized this. Crockett recalled Marilyn Townsend showing him the charges against her son, and "where they were going to have to go to court, and she said, 'Now, thank God, Crockett, the home is in Anafuel's name.'

"And she says, 'Now, we've got to get the stock out of David's name and divide it amongst the boys, so that if we lose the case, they don't take the stock.'

"She said, 'They can't touch the house.'"

The Townsends were convinced that so long as they personally owned little or nothing and kept their major possessions in the name of their corporation, they could not be successfully sued. Financially penalties brought against the family for their negligence would not have to be paid. They could declare bankruptcy because of their high personal debt, yet continue living as they had been, with Anafuel paying their expenses, officially owning their home, and otherwise protecting them.

I don't know what I expected. Compassion, perhaps. Horror at the thought of what their son had done and what Dwayne would be experiencing for the rest of his life. Something more than a family whose concern was the protection of assets, not the rebuilding of shattered lives.

But there was nothing.

◆ ◆ ◆

When David Townsend moved to Houston it was a necessity. The trial had gone well for his son, but business had gone badly for him. "We didn't have an office because we didn't have a cash flow and we couldn't pay rent," David Crockett explained. "So we were working wherever we could get together on the phone and sit down in some restaurant drinking coffee, occasionally over at Townsend's home. But we ended up forming a plan that we would attempt to get out of California and come to Houston, Texas, because Houston, Texas, was the gasoline capital of the world. And if we were going to be in the business, this would be a good place to start, because the bureaucratic agencies and rules and regulations were not as strict as they were in the State of California."

The corporation created for blending fuel in Texas was called Petrolife, Incorporated. This effectively eliminated the involvement of both stockholders and investors in Anafuel, even though the additive and the business were the same. Originally, the idea was to form a partnership with the five Maxwell brothers from a city called Denvers, Texas, and the Anafuel Corporation of America. At least fifty percent of the proceeds from the new business would go back into Anafuel, paying stockholders and the directors. But David Townsend wanted more money, so he eliminated Crockett and the others from the new corporation.

"So here we are in Houston, Texas, and I just came from being an executive vice president, a director, a stockholder and an officer, a secretary and treasurer of Anafuel Corporation, and I am now, on Monday morning, an employee of a new company," Crockett explained.

According to Crockett, David Townsend again bought a home using Anafuel Corporation of America checks. There was no money in the account, and the owner of the house had him evicted after three months of living in the home. "Here again he's going to buy a home with corporate money in the name of

Anafuel, but it ain't in the name of Anafuel, his home. It's the Townsend home. He's already saying, 'Mark, this is your room. Jeff, this is your room.'"

The checks were issued by Townsend and signed by Townsend, and always without the approval of the Anafuel board.

In addition to the bad checks, Townsend was working other scams, according to Crockett, who became an informant for the Internal Revenue Service. As Crockett explained, Petrolife, the new Texas company, "had applied for a tax-free exemption status with the Treasury Department for purchase and sale of our product.

"At my request, the IRS representative visited our office here in Houston to discuss that. And at this meeting, the Maxwells, specifically Lloyd Maxwell, determined that the IRS wanted too much information that Maxwell Brothers considered to be personal and private in nature, that they did not want to divulge to the IRS." Instead, Lloyd Maxwell gave the form to Crockett to keep, saying that if they decided to get the exemption at a later date, they could apply for it.

Crockett said David Townsend wanted the exemption because it would ultimately mean more money for the company. According to Crockett, Townsend later took the form from him, created his own number, and proceeded to use the forged form to make purchases. It was then that David Crockett felt he had to turn in his boss and one-time friend. But even with all these problems, David Townsend, his family, and his insurance company seemed still determined to fight any compensation for Dwayne.

Chapter XI

CHOICES

There are moments in every life when you are confronted by darkness, a darkness that may force you to make choices that challenge the values you claim to profess. You spend years telling people that you would ***never*** steal, then one day, faced with mounting bills despite working two physically exhausting jobs, you find a purse at a bus stop. No one will see you take the money that is inside it—money that will meet your immediate needs and leave you with a small cushion. Yet there is also ample identification to be able to return it.

Suddenly "never" takes on a different meaning. You have come face to face with the moment when you will discover whether or not you really believe what you profess. Until that instant, the issue of stealing has been an abstract one. Now it is a serious consideration. It is at times like these that you learn a lesson about yourself you may not wish to know.

There are numerous other examples, of course. A woman solemnly declares that she would never cheat on a spouse. Then years pass, the couple either starts taking the relationship for granted or become estranged through lack of communication, and gradually there is an uneasiness. When another person comes along being open, friendly, respectful, and attractive, there is a good chance an affair will be considered if both parties are interested. Not that the affair is pre-ordained—it is not. Rather it is considered, and the decision tells far more about the morality of the individual than any promises made during the throes of the honeymoon stage.

So it was with Mark and me when the truth about Dwayne's injuries hit us. We suddenly had to confront an aspect of ourselves we never previously wanted to admit was present.

Mark had taken time off from work during the first few days after the shooting. But he was self-employed. One of our sons helped out with service calls, and our daughter-in-law volunteered to help with the telephone. However, Mark was the expert in the family, the man who could do more work more efficiently than anyone else on whom we could rely for help. He had to be in the field or we would not be able to afford any of the expenses we would soon be incurring. Although it had hurt us deeply, we already had to apply for help under Medicaid. We had taken pride in paying our own way for everything, yet now we had to rely upon the state program for those essentially without finances. Having returned to California and begun a new business, we did not yet have insurance coverage because we were between policies. Everything was wrong, and the only way we could begin to get back in control was for Mark to work. Dwayne understood, but Mark still spent several hours a day at the hospital.

It was only days after returning to his service calls that Mark came home with the offer that should have been unthinkable. One of our customers, a gentle, loving man who cared deeply about our family, had a business in an area surrounded by people who earned their living in violation of the law. Some were thieves, others were engaged in crimes of physical violence such as extortion and loansharking enforcement. They did not bother our customer, and he did not have dealings with them other than in the course of being a merchant in the area. But he knew who they were, and he was so outraged by our pain that he made discreet inquiries as to what they would charge to hurt or kill Jeff Townsend. Then he went to Mark and told him that because of our circumstances, a "hit" could be obtained for around two thousand dollars. Since the going rate at the time was ten thousand dollars, as we later learned from law enforcement sources, it was obvious that even the racketeers had compassion in their own perverted way.

We could afford two thousand dollars. It was a lot of money, given the horrendous medical bills we were facing. However, we could find ways to earn the cash needed. And given what Jeff had done to Dwayne, it seemed a small price to pay.

We had been watching Dwayne's struggles; listening to his optimism based on childlike naïveté. He informed us that he was going to be walking in a year. He was determined to heal. Yet he was angry in rehab. He did not like some of the staff, and he became belligerent and uncooperative. Some of his reasons were valid, such as a support person who deliberately tried to physically hurt him as her way of "teaching" him to have a better attitude. I thought Dwayne was making up the complaint until I caught her actually bending back his fingers as punishment. I was certain Dwayne was not the only one with whom she was taking improper action; apparently the administrative staff agreed. After an investigation into our complaint, she was fired. But her termination did not make Dwayne a better patient. He was an adolescent facing a horrendous situation. He believed—had to believe—he was going to recover completely and had very definite ideas of how things were going to be, and his stay was not happening his way.

What Dwayne did not understand, but we did, was that the staff was working on a range of motion exercises meant to keep his limbs capable of movement, his recovery a possibility. Muscles can atrophy, and other damage can occur which can be irreversible. Efforts were made to keep his hands from permanently closing into fists, for example, since that is a common problem with a spinal cord injury.

But such therapy was really just "busy work." The diagnosis of complete quadriplegia made during the first forty-eight hours after Dwayne was shot seemed to be the one that was accurate. Dwayne would need someone to care for him the rest of his life. The friend that had shot him, Jeff Townsend, could lead a normal existence. We could not help our hostility. At the very least, we wanted Jeff Townsend to know the same pain and helplessness he had inflicted upon our son for the rest of his life.

Mark and I discussed the contract killing, though I did not realize Mark was thinking of taking vengeance himself. Mark's own pain was enormous, pain he did not want to discuss with me because he knew how much I was suffering. He seriously considered taking the shotgun from the locked cabinet in which it was stored, buying ammunition, and shooting Jeff Townsend.

Although I was not aware of how often Mark went to look at the gun cabinet, periodically he would walk over to the gun cabinet and look at the weapons he had secured inside. Sometimes he would look for a few seconds. Other times he would spend more time just staring. He seemed to be weighing the actions he might take. He was not aware of anyone watching him, being lost in thought about what he might do. And always he walked away, not opening the cabinet, not touching the weapons. Yet for several weeks he could not stop considering the possibility of either killing Jeff or destroying his kneecaps so he would never be able to walk again. In our hurt and pain we considered every possibility for revenge. We explored what only a few weeks earlier would have been unthinkable.

We were nice, normal, moral, upright people, hard working and devoted to a service business. We were not prone to violence. We were not people who saw vengeance as a way of handling our problems. Dwayne's favorite meal was my creamed chipped beef on toast. My favorite way to relax was with a tall glass of milk enjoyed while sitting quietly in a rocking chair. We were what urban residents often call "white bread."

Although I tried to tell myself that we weren't serious in our desire to have Jeff Townsend maimed, crippled, or killed, the truth is that we were. Perhaps it was a stage of grieving. Perhaps all of us must face certain moral and ethical issues in our lives, especially in times of crisis. All I know is that I did think about such actions, weighing all possible consequences before recognizing that I was incapable of deliberately causing such pain to another person. We finally made the only decision we could—the choice to let the legal system deal with Jeff Townsend and his family.

Why did we make that decision? Mark was one reason—we loved him and needed him. I had to have his strength and emotional support. His absence would have caused us financial hardship, of course, but we could have survived without his earnings. It was his strong presence in all our lives, his unlimited, unconditional love, his inherent goodness. All of that would be lost if he went to jail for either his own actions or for hiring someone to hurt or murder Jeff Townsend.

Then there was the moral issue. Morality, not law, was the greatest factor in our decision. We wanted Jeff to suffer; I still want Jeff Townsend to have a deeply troubled life. But we knew that it was not for us to be the cause of whatever was to happen to him. Jeff's immediate fate would be and should have been in the hands of the legal system. Ultimately, he would answer to God. At the moment we had more important concerns, and they involved trying to get Dwayne through those traumatic weeks.

Chapter XII

STRENGTHS AND WEAKNESSES

Dwayne McKee's greatest strength was the hospital personnel's greatest nightmare. He accepted the need for the drugs and additional therapy needed to combat the clots. But beyond that, he never tried to adjust to anything, including the routine required for his care. He felt that the trauma he had endured was one that should be conquered. Perhaps seeing his future in their failures, he could not tolerate the weakness in others and was determined to have them conquer their problems. He longed to prove he would ultimately triumph.

This made him impatient with other patients who were complacent. For example, there was one young man who was what is known as an incomplete quadriplegic—he had a small amount of motor control of his lower body, though not enough to be meaningful. Dwayne, even at fourteen, felt that you could build on what you had. The other boy focused on what he had lost, not only refusing to help himself but influencing those around him. His mother did not push him, nor did she bother buying him a wheelchair when he was released from the hospital. Instead, the youth was pushed about in a shopping cart, an experience that was undoubtedly extremely humiliating.

Whenever he could convince someone to push him, or when he had access to an electric wheelchair whose controls he could work with his head, Dwayne visited the other patients. He encouraged them, realizing that his presence could make a difference. It was then that he decided that as soon as he could return to school he would become a psychologist. He told himself he would be walking by then, though he knew that the profession was one he could practice even if confined to a chair. All he needed was his good mind, compassion, and the training to know what to say and how to say it.

But despite these lofty aims, Dwayne was also becoming a "monster." As the only young adolescent in rehab, he was a nuisance for the staff.

Everything about rehab was wrong in Dwayne's mind. He wanted me to spend the night with him, hoping I would protect him from the tests conducted at two o'clock in the morning by the support staff. In truth, he was safe and well cared for, but he was frightened of being out of control in a strange environment for which he had no preparation.

He became easily angered by people on the staff, and as much as Dwayne loved his mother, I was also the person closest to him when he wanted to lash out at the world. I was vulnerable to his emotions, and he knew it. He would verbally fight with me, expressing his frustration in the only way he knew how.

Dwayne was also difficult for the therapists to deal with. He learned to utilize his shoulders enough to move his useless arms, yet progress was achieved only with constant fights. Dwayne would talk about the fact that he was going to walk out of the hospital soon. Then he would refuse to work with the therapists as they tried to teach him to use a manual wheelchair.

The electric wheelchair was easy for him. The control could be operated with very limited movement. But a standard wheelchair required him to push with wrists and arms since he had no control of his hands. The effort for movement was enormous, exhausting him each time he propelled himself forward. He insisted that he could not do what was asked because he became too tired too quickly. They tried to explain that he would become stronger from the practice, that he needed to achieve whatever motor skills were possible.

Dwayne learned to use a standard, though extremely lightweight, wheelchair in the manner the staff desired. Yet it came only with a fight, and once he had mastered such movement, he used his new limited body control against the staff. He jammed his crippled hands into the spokes of the wheelchair instead of using them for propulsion whenever he did not want to be moved. This occurred most frequently when the rehab staff wanted him to go into the hospital swimming pool, where he did not feel safe. He was protected and carefully watched, and the staff knew that in the water disabled people were more mobile than they were when out of it. Yet Dwayne refused to have such therapy without a fight, knowing he could be injured by his own resistance.

The problem was that quadriplegics have spasms that, at first, are uncontrollable. The movements are intense, painfully stretching the muscles. Even worse, Dwayne's legs began spasming as soon as he sensed the water. Although the water was kept at a carefully controlled, perfectly safe temperature, Dwayne said it felt to him like thousands of tiny knife blades touching his body at the same time. He did not care that the pool therapy was good for him. He did not care that it might speed whatever healing was possible. He just knew that he hated it, and he fought the staff, crying, calling them names, telling them to "go to hell" when they tried working with him.

There were no apologies on the part of the staff. There was no sympathy for the boy. They had a job to do, and that was to assure that Dwayne obtained the greatest possible use of his body, whatever that meant. The fact that he did not understand, that he often refused to cooperate, was ignored. They simply noted his failure to adjust to the therapy on his chart.

At some point during the first few weeks there seemed to be open warfare between Dwayne and the staff. They took a clipboard, placed his daily schedule on the board, and then began noting his actions. Was he on time for therapy? Was he late? Did he fail to show up? Each action was duly noted and signed by the appropriate staff member. He had an ongoing record, like a child's report card.

One possibility was that they were protecting themselves against a lawsuit if he did not improve in any way. The notations would indicate that he was scheduled for a proper range of therapeutic activities. It would also indicate that the failure to receive the routine care came from Dwayne's deliberate actions, not their negligence.

Another possibility was that they thought the clipboard approach, with its implied reprimand for failure to comply, would make Dwayne more cooperative. He would feel like a small child, not a teenager on the verge of manhood. He would cooperate rather than face what they might have hoped would feel like humiliation. Whatever the reason, Dwayne did start cooperating with the staff. Yet the staff still did not relate to Dwayne.

One psychiatrist kept checking on him randomly, trying to talk about his psychological problems. Dwayne did not wish to talk with her. He felt that what she was discussing did not relate to his needs. Eventually, he used foul language to tell her that he didn't have a head problem. "Look, I have a leg problem. I can't walk and I'm determined to leave this damn place on foot."

Finally a conference was called. Dwayne's doctor was angry with him. Some of the nurses were angry with him. And some of the therapists were angry with him. We were summoned to a conference to discuss Dwayne's failings, and it was in that conference that Mark exploded.

Mark walked up front and all the anger inside him spilled out. "Hey, what do you people think you're doing here? Picture yourself being fourteen years old and losing your arms and legs. Put yourself in this child's position, and I'd like to see how in the hell you guys can handle it before you make any more of these fucking comments.

"I don't buy this bullshit. I'm not going to go along with it. Some of you people got all of your faculties, and to me *you're* not handling it very damn good.

"*You're* not being very goddamned understandable here. Give the goddamned kid a chance. He's lost his goddamned arms and his legs. He hasn't lost his head, you know? I'm not going to buy this. I'm just not going to put up with it."

Mark sat down, still furious. Later he told me, "They were trying to be God and jury and everything else, and the therapists were turning him in, and getting his ass in trouble because he wouldn't go along with everything they wanted."

Mark's language may have been crude, but his anger was intense and seemed to get the point across. The therapists had been trained a certain way, but most of them refused to look at the patient. They wanted to force Dwayne to perform like a textbook case. They didn't want to work with his psychological needs and desires. There was no harm in his attempting to use his body instead of mastering special mechanical devices. If he succeeded at something, such as getting his arms through his shirt, and if he did it differently than their approach called for, what harm was done? He had pride in his own success, and the end result was the same. He learned to do a task that would ultimately help him lead an independent life. The staff hadn't seen it that way.

But Mark's actions worked. Dwayne was made aware of his father's harsh anger. He realized that his father was supporting him, regardless of what that meant. Mark had the patience to let Dwayne try and fail, if only because he also knew that in trying, Dwayne just might succeed.

The action brought father and son much closer. It also caused both Dwayne and the staff to reconsider their feud. Dwayne became more cooperative, rebelling in ways that were more tolerable and far less frequent. The staff worked with Dwayne, watching progress that was at least as good as they could expect from anyone. They probably both learned a lesson, though in reviewing some of Dwayne's hospital records and psychological evaluations, it was obvious that the staff would not be sorry to see him leave when he could be released to our care.

◆ ◆ ◆

Day after day there were many difficult lessons for all of us to learn. Dwayne was wearing special pressure stockings that helped with his circulation. He had a diet he hated, though we were allowed to go to a nearby restaurant. There were also special outings to a movie theater equipped to handle the extremely disabled. Mark and I often accompanied Dwayne and the others.

The physical therapy was rigorous, lasting from nine in the morning until noon. His limbs were worked through a full range of motion, something I was taught to assist in doing with him so I could handle matters when he came home. There were hand exercises. He had to learn to pick up blocks to move his arms. Activities were adapted to whatever he could do with his body. When he was incapable of movement, machines took over to assure exercise. He would be strapped onto an electric stationary bicycle, for example, the motor working the pedals and turning the wheel. He received the benefits of riding a bicycle even though he was physically unable to handle the work.

There was a special pulley and weight device called a rickshaw. There was an arm machine. Everything was planned around the idea of giving him as much mobility as possible.

Occupational therapy lasted several hours after lunch. He was taught how to get his shirt on. He learned ways to lean forward, dangling his arms into sleeves, then pulling the shirt over his head.

There were several mechanical devices available to help Dwayne with the routine tasks of daily living. However, he was determined to not use them if at all possible. He wanted to be certain that he kept himself as normal as he could. He was convinced that only in such a manner would he heal.

Chapter XIII

SILLY REQUESTS

One day several weeks later, Dwayne's indomitable will seemed to triumph. "Will you pay me one hundred dollars to move my big toe?" he asked me over the phone laughing. It was a silly request, but my heart clutched at what seemed the unlikelyhood of this. How could Dwayne move his toe? His body was useless. Perhaps he had just wanted to call me. The hospital equipped patients like Dwayne with a special telephone containing large buttons and a receiver rest that enabled them to work the system with their heads if necessary. Making telephone calls, even pointless ones, helped him feel somewhat independent.

"Of course I'll pay you the money," I told him. Then I hung up, sighed heavily, and went back to work. A short time later I gathered up my things and went to the hospital for my daily visit.

"I have something to show you," Dwayne said. He was in his wheelchair, his right foot exposed. I looked down as he requested, and to my astonishment, his big toe moved up and down.

I screamed with excitement and hugged Dwayne, whose grin reached from ear to ear. "I'm going to call your dad and Kimberly to tell them." I must have been louder than I thought, because nurses came over to see what was happening.

The nurses ran to see Dwayne's accomplishment, and he proudly repeated the action of raising and lowering his big toe.

It was a smooth movement, controlled. I was laughing, crying, hugging him. "About my check . . . " he said. So I made out a check for one hundred dollars, which he said he planned to use to buy baseball cards.

"I've been suckered into paying you," I laughed, thinking I would have given him a thousand times that much if I had had it. Our eyes met. We did not need words. After all the pain, for the first time since Jeff Townsend called to tell us that Dwayne had been shot, there was hope.

Dr. Rosen called the incident "controlled spasticity" when Dwayne showed him the skill. Doctors know that quadriplegics experiencing spasms can learn to use their minds to slow or stop the painful, involuntary spasms. He was certain that was what Dwayne had done.

But it wasn't. Dwayne knew it and I knew it. He moved his toe when he wished to do so. He did it deliberately when asked. He did not move it at any other time. Perhaps he would never control any other part of his body. All I knew was that if a big toe could move, why not the whole foot? And if the foot could be made to move, the potential was unlimited.

Dwayne felt the same way. Dr. Rosen could be as pessimistic as he wished to be. He was not going to remove the pleasure we felt for the achievement Dwayne had accomplished. We were depressed by his terrible bedside manner. However, for the first time we felt there was reason to hope, not just live in fear.

◆ ◆ ◆

It was in August that Dwayne moved forward another step. I had gone to the hospital to have lunch with him. He was in his wheelchair, and as we finished eating, he leaned back against his cervical collar as though trying to relax. Then his right arm rose slowly, the back of his hand lightly rubbing against his forehead before it flopped down in his lap. He could not control the movement beyond the raising and lowering of his bent hand, but he could do that much! I don't know if it took more control than moving his toe. I did not care to ask. We had been told that his body would never again respond to the signals his mind tried to send through the spinal cord, the nerves, and the muscles.

I was thrilled. For a boy who had once been an athlete, the limited movement was intensely frustrating. But Dwayne was no longer an athlete; the shooting had left him with a young adult's mind in a body more helpless than that of a newborn. To see him control his arm even in such a crude manner was a thrill that brought tears to my eyes. I shouted for joy. It was a moment of great happiness, of shared triumph.

◆ ◆ ◆

The hospital professionals were more subdued in their reaction. They felt the limited movements Dwayne had achieved were not a breakthrough. There are degrees of quadriplegic abilities. Some victims of severe spinal cord injuries have flawless minds and useless bodies. Their abilities are no different from those of the human heads kept alive in the laboratories of mad scientists in early science fiction and horror movies. They are capable of a full range of emotions. They lose none of their intellectual abilities. Yet they can never again handle the most basic human functions without help.

At the other extreme are partial quadriplegics. They may be able to move their fingers enough to learn to use a computer keyboard. They may have limited arm or leg movement. They can feed themselves with utensils they can control without someone having to attach a special Velcro holder or other device. They can handle matters of personal hygiene. They can develop enough strength and control to move themselves slowly and carefully in a standard wheelchair, but will never be able to stand and dance with a lover. They can have a child and hold that child in their arms, though they will probably never be able to lift the child off the ground. They can live independently of a trained care taker and hold a variety of jobs that require very limited dexterity.

Between the two extremes are the patients who have some motor skills. Perhaps they can operate a keyboard with one hand, or two or three fingers. Perhaps they stand briefly, bracing themselves on parallel bars or some other support. The abilities may help them obtain a job, or they may be only of psychological value, such as being able to move a single toe as Dwayne did that wonderful day in the hospital.

Whatever the patient's circumstances, the staff recognizes that the person will face a life of frustration, of unfulfilled hope, of possible ridicule or unwanted pity. They will have great anger, bouts of depression, perhaps periods of grandiose plans countered by the realization that they are not in control of their healing.

Being a quadriplegic is not a condition overcome by positive thinking, mind over matter, or endless exercise. No matter what skills may be developed, they are never enough. The victim will always be severely limited compared with the past he or she had known.

The hospital staff applauded Dwayne's triumphs. They delighted in his moments of happiness. But they felt there would be no miracles. They refused to offer hope or what they felt was false promise. Based on past experience, they could not encourage him to believe in a life they were sure he would never experience.

But Dwayne and our family refused to give up hope. By September it was obvious that Dwayne had made enough progress to return home full time. We had taken him out to dinner. We had brought him home for brief breaks from the hospital's routine. We had arranged for the help he needed, as well as being trained to assist in those areas that did not require a professional.

Dwayne had learned to utilize his body as best he could in occupational therapy. He learned to eat using special eating utensils attached to his wrists with Velcro devices. However, he did so only reluctantly. Although his movements were awkward and lacked the skills that even a small child brings to eating, he wanted to be able to eat with his hands, not an artificial device.

There was a small kitchen in the occupational room where Dwayne was taught to use the refrigerator and oven. He was able to make pretzels, an achievement that delighted him. He also found that with a special stand for holding cards, he could play gin and other games. He also was able to very slowly move a peg into a hole in the manner of a toddler learning shapes and sizes.

We knew where Dwayne had started after the shooting and were thrilled with the hope his achievements implied. Dwayne saw where he had been before the shooting and was angry with his inabilities. However, he had learned a degree of patience, was no longer so hostile to the staff, and was now telling everyone that he would be walking on his sixteenth birthday. Since he was fourteen-and-a-half at the time, the goal was more realistic than his comments about leaving the hospital on foot.

◆ ◆ ◆

There were many steps to be taken in preparation for Dwayne's return, from modifying our home to learning special care procedures. He could not work the muscles that made his bladder and sphincter function. Without a daily catheterization, for example, urine would build up and poison his body.

The issue of bodily functions was perhaps the most humiliating for Dwayne, though he accepted his problems without complaint. He was in his early teens, making the transition from child to man. He had been physically ready for sexual activity before he was shot, though he was raised in a manner that meant we expected him to wait for emotional maturity in a totally committed relationship. Yet he was keenly aware of the dual role of the penis—for urination and for the pleasurable experience of intercourse—as any adolescent in the throes of puberty. Privacy had become important to him. He expected all of us to respect his need to handle bodily functions alone, as would anyone his age or older.

The spinal cord damage erased any chance for privacy. Dwayne had lost sphincter and bladder control. His urine leaked out throughout the day, yet he never fully voided his bladder. Anything that remained more than twenty-four hours would cause a urinary tract infection that could easily kill him. There had been one time when he had such an infection in the hospital, and all of us were concerned that it not happen again. Yet until he could urinate on his own—an ability that might never return—he had to be catheterized daily.

The technique was a simple one, yet very difficult for everyone. Normally there was a rubber tube, one end of which slipped over the penis, the other end of which went into a leg bag. Most of the urine would pass through the tube and into the bag. However, once a day I had to use a special kit designed for the purpose of helping someone lacking such control. I would open the kit and scrub my hands with antiseptic soap, just like a doctor preparing for surgery. I would put on sterile gloves, then open sterile packages containing a catheter and a lubricant that made its insertion easier. Finally, I would slowly push it into the urethra until at least a drop of urine flowed back. Sometimes that was all that remained in the bladder. At other times there was a much larger quantity that came out.

Bowel movements were a different matter. Again, once a day he would need help voiding excrement. He would have to be moved onto his side, then braced so he could stay in that position. I had to place special eighteen-by-twenty-four-inch pads designed for absorbing body waste underneath him. Then, after washing and putting on the sterile gloves, I would insert a suppository, then cover him with a sheet. He would lay on the bed until he sensed his bowels were moving. Then the pads, covered with waste, would be removed and replaced with others while we waited to see if there was more to come. Sometimes the staff said the pads had to be removed only once. Sometimes three or four sets had to be used. Only when it was over could I clean Dwayne and let him gather his dignity for another twenty-four hours.

The procedure was messy but necessary. Dwayne accepted the fact that his mother would have to be involved with what should have been a private act. Part of him had returned to infancy, and my awareness of that fact made handling the job a loving act, not one that revolted me. Yet Dwayne knew that there was reason to believe I would be repeating the procedures seven days a week, fifty-two weeks a year, year in and year out until I became too old and infirm for the task. Then someone else would have to take over. Unless there was a change in his condition, he would go through life dependent upon others for the most basic of bodily functions.

Dwayne was never so concerned as we were because he had not lived long enough to understand what he was facing. He did not seem at all uncomfortable with my practice attempts and his father's observations as they trained us in the hospital. He seemed to feel that our actions meant that he was one step closer to coming home. We could not help thinking unless matters changed, though, he would come to an understanding later. He might suffer rejection by a woman he wanted to make his wife. He might be restricted in the work he could do. His living arrangement might require at least a part-time attendant. Yet all that mattered to him was coming home.

And at that point Dwayne's return was what mattered most to us as well. He would be doing physical therapy from home, both with a specialist who would come to our house daily and in our swimming pool. We bought a special shower chair and were in the process of enlarging doorways, installing special ramped equipment, and otherwise creating an atmosphere where his movements would not be restricted.

We also learned to use a sliding board, something we all hoped Dwayne would be able to handle on his own one day. The board might be considered an ultra-slippery, super-hard plastic shoe horn. However, instead of being used to ease your foot into a tight shoe, the sliding board was meant to move Dwayne from one sitting position to another.

The sliding board was approximately thirty inches long and maybe eight or ten inches wide. It would be placed under his rear end, then onto the seat to which he was being transferred. Anyone helping him could readily move him cross the board from a car seat to a wheelchair, or from the wheelchair to the shower chair—wherever. Lifting him meant trying to lift dead weight at what was often an awkward angle. Any assistant, no matter how strong, was at risk of having a back injury. Thus the sliding board, which some quadriplegics are eventually able to use themselves, becomes a critical tool for mobility.

One of the more crucial modifications to the bathroom was the installation of a temperature control device on the water pipes. Dwayne's skin was sensitive to the air, yet he could not sense the degree of cold or heat when immersed in water. It would be very easy for him to be scalded by water splashing the lower part of his body without his realizing the temperature was too high.

The most time-consuming part of caring for Dwayne would be dressing him. He was regularly having involuntary leg and foot spasms. Each time his toes would bend straight up, as though someone was deliberately pulling them back in order to hurt him. The pain was intense. Whoever was helping him dress had to physically force the toes back down.

The problems with his feet meant that Dwayne would have to wear oversized tennis shoes. He would also need extra time to dress because getting enough control of his feet for the socks and shoes to be placed on them required an average of twenty minutes of work.

Ultimately it was found that Dwayne needed approximately five hours of help a day for basic survival. Since I handled the business calls from our home, it made sense that I be the one to work with him, supported by professionals when necessary. For me, the sacrifice was a minor one. Dwayne was coming home. He was alive. What we could not know was for how long.

Chapter XIV

MANY KINDS OF ANGER

Our anger was different now. It was driven by a desire for revenge, to create circumstances that would somehow fit the Biblical concept of an eye for an eye, of punishment that fits the crime.

This was something more, a combination of feelings that I think we all knew would be with us for years to come, so we tended to deny them.

Mark was probably the most comfortable with his anger. He was willing to talk about it, to curse, to speak about his hostility to the Townsends and the results of Jeff's shooting of Dwayne.

Dwayne and I were the least comfortable expressing ourselves. Dwayne wanted me to know that he loved me, that he appreciated the time I devoted to his care. He kept talking about his plans for his future, speaking positively about walking again in the future. He knew his belief that he would walk from the hospital wasn't possible, so he changed his stated goal to his sixteenth birthday.

Yet Dwayne had almost as many doubts as the doctors. He also hated the deformities caused by the paralysis, hated his limitations. He took out his anger indirectly, being extraordinarily demanding of my time and hypercritical of everything I did that was not "perfect." I was with him almost constantly each day, so I was the easy target for his frustrations.

Dwayne also reacted internally. Each time he had to deal with what happened, such as when he was being interviewed by the lawyers handling the lawsuit, or when he saw Jeff or the Townsends, his stomach became upset. Soon he developed an ulcer. "It's just stress," he would say. "Everybody has it."

Then one day he was leaning over the side of his wheelchair and began vomiting blood. The blood splattered his clothing, the arm of the chair, and the floor. I was horrified and called our doctor. He was able to stop it within twelve hours, and since then the ulcer has been controlled with special medication.

What Dwayne would not face was that most people handle stress without a bleeding ulcer. He also did not know how frightened his ulcer made me. I was not only watching my son in crisis, I was remembering the death of my father.

My father was an intensely gentle man, an employee of ABC Studios, a man who never fought with anyone, never expressed anger even when wronged. The trouble was that he did feel anger and did have problems that he was too polite to express. He internalized all his feelings, the intensity of his emotions churning stomach acids that eventually created a perforated ulcer.

He was only fifty-one when I received a frantic telephone call from my mother. She told me that he was in the bathroom doubled over the tub, vomiting large quantities of blood. By the time I arrived, the ambulance had rushed him to a hospital where he kept trying to insist he would be all right. They knew otherwise, frantically giving him transfusions because they could not stop the blood loss and had to try to keep him from going into shock. He finally consented to surgery that night, but it was too late. His body was overwhelmed by the trauma. I received a call at home at 2:00 A.M. telling me he was dead.

My stress was also intense, though my outlet became a domestic one. I made bread.

I had always wanted to make bread, but I never really had the energy to do it right. The dough is thick and difficult to work with, like a modeling clay on the verge of becoming too dry to handle. You knead it, then turn it a quarter turn and knead some more. The harder and longer you work, the softer the bread. The finished loaf represents hard physical labor, especially when it is done by hand, as I was doing it.

Before Dwayne was shot, my efforts resulted in bread that had the texture of rocks. Dwayne could have taken a loaf to use as a puck during his games of street hockey, and except for the shape and size, no one would have known the difference.

I returned to breadmaking because it was something I could do after Dwayne returned home while he was resting. It also seemed a good outlet for my physical restlessness. Yet the bread became something more.

The first day I made a loaf of bread, I had been looking at Dwayne. He was the youngest of our children, yet he was almost his full adult height. He would grow some more. His voice would deepen. His body would fill out. But he was on the edge of manhood, strong, active, agile, bright, and popular with the boys and girls in his class. He was also the sensitive one, the person to whom the other kids turned when they had a problem that they needed a trusted friend to help them solve.

Mark and I had thought that Dwayne and Kimberly would

soon be leaving home. We supposed we would be at a time in our lives when we could reduce the day-to-day struggle. We would only be financially responsible for our own future, and we could cut back, relocate to be near one or more of our children, travel, or do anything else we pleased. We could become somewhat selfish because we would no longer have any dependents.

Our long-range plans had to change, however, because when we took Dwayne home from the hospital it was as though we were bringing a baby home from the maternity ward. Once again we experienced the nights of constant interruption, though instead of colic, frequent feeding demands, or other forms of restlessness, we had to turn Dwayne's body every two hours, twenty-four hours a day, seven days a week. If we failed to turn him, he would develop bed sores. If he developed bed sores, the resulting infection would likely be so serious he would have to return to the hospital. If the infection did not heal quickly, his reduced immune system would cause him to deteriorate and die.

At first we arranged for a nurse to help us from 11:00 P.M. to 7:00 A.M., but one of the earliest discoveries we made about caring for a quadriplegic is that once you leave the surroundings of a hospital or extended care facility, the quality of available help varies widely. A large staff assures careful supervision. Not only are the employees carefully screened, but anyone lax is quickly discovered by a co-worker. This is not true when you hire an individual, as we learned as the people who came to work for us kept falling asleep. Dwayne never got into trouble, and for all I know they were able to rouse themselves in time to help him. However, when I got up at night to check on Dwayne and found the person sleeping, I was horrified. Mark and I decided to take over full responsibility without such assistance.

Again I withheld my anger with "professionals" who were ignoring my son's needs. Instead, I told myself that our awakening every two hours made sense. After all these nights, I regularly found myself not really sleeping, worrying that Dwayne might be mishandled by or scared with strangers. I also feared that he might awaken with nightmares about the shooting, needing Mark or me for reassurance. There were endless reasons to check on him, and my rest would have been as limited with help as without. Or so I tried to make myself believe.

There were other radical changes causing hardship in our lives. The catheterization was done each evening. A home tutor was sent by the Board of Education. Physical and occupational therapy took place each day. There were seemingly endless prescriptions to fill and refill, special kits we had to buy, and the rest of the family's needs to consider.

Dwayne was also exhausted. He had not known a full night's sleep since he was in the hospital. His body needed rest, and both his body and mind craved sleep for healing and, perhaps, a time to forget the constant struggle to achieve even the simplest of movements.

Dwayne was embarrassed by the waste collection devices on his body, yet he forced himself to go out to the home of some friends which had been decorated with "Welcome Home" signs, balloons, and similar objects. There was pizza and soda. There were songs. And everyone ignored the fact that Dwayne was strapped into a wheelchair, his loose-fitting sweat pants positioned to hide the urine bag he was wearing.

The normal plans, hopes, and dreams of parents about to experience the "empty nest" after spending decades raising children were abandoned. Jeff Townsend had robbed us of options, and the first time I went into the kitchen to make bread, my heart was filled with the pain of this realization. I took great pride in each small triumph Dwayne achieved, yet the truth seemed obvious. Dwayne was probably going to be confined to a wheelchair, his body severely limited, for the rest of his life.

Angry and weary, I made my dough and started to knead. I

thought of Jeff, the boy who had been Dwayne's friend and almost constant companion for so many months before the shooting. I thought of our son. And I worked the bread, turning it a quarter turn, then kneading it again.

The bread was like a fairy tale's enchanted mirror, suddenly filled with the faces of the Townsends and the memories of Dwayne's struggles to move even one toe. The kneading became harder, more intense. The dough was Jeff's face, and my hands pushed and pulled, ripping the flesh and crushing the skull created by my imagination.

Tears fell steadily, their saltiness burning the corners of my eyes before they fell onto the dough. I blinked rapidly, wiping the wetness with the backs of my hands. I did not want the liquid to ruin the dough.

There was a controlled frenzy to my efforts. Push, pull, roll, twist, and turn the dough another quarter turn. I was a wrestler pummeling a long-time enemy I finally had on the mat in a match which only one competitor could survive.

Knead the dough. Turn it a quarter turn. Knead it again.

I heard strange sounds in the kitchen, and I paused for a moment to make certain Dwayne was not trying to call my name. Then I realized that the sounds were those of my sobbing, and I fought the display of emotion, fearing that if my crying became any more intense, I would be unable to stop.

I returned to the task I had set out to do. I had to knead the dough. I had to make the bread. I had to give my family a gift of normality in a world gone mad.

The bread I made was conceived in love, kneaded in anger, and flavored with salty tears; it was a recipe of grief and thanksgiving. Perhaps this was the bread of the Old Testament of people in exile. I used leavening; they did not. Yet surely their women wept as I did, praising God for the survival of their loved ones while mourning the wounded, the maimed, and the crippled whose valiant battles assured their existence.

Over those months I don't know how many loaves of bread I made that shared the same recipe. The kitchen was the place to which I could retreat to weep in private. I did not want Dwayne to see my pain for fear of adding to his own. I did not want Mark to bear the burden of trying to comfort me when there was no comfort possible, just raw emotion that could not and should not be contained within my heart.

Eventually there were no more tears. Eventually there was an acceptance of my son's condition, of a future of limitations, of hope tempered by reality. Yet the anger did not leave me, and when my family compliments me on the quality of the bread I make, on how delicious it is, I just nod. For within me I know it has been kneaded with the memory of Jeff Townsend's face firmly implanted on the dough.

Right: Dwayne McKee, age fourteen, on his first day of junior high school.

Below: Dwayne with his "best friend," thirteen-year-old Jeffrey Townsend, taken not long before Jeffrey shot Dwayne with his father's gun.

Bottom: Hale Junior High Choir. Dwayne is sixth from left middle row. After the shooting, the choir would sing a special song for their classmate at their graduation ceremony.

Left: The Townsend Family's Candlewood home, where the shooting occurred.

Below: A police photograph of the scene of the shooting: David and Mariyn's bedroom as seen from the doorway. Dwayne's blood-soaked shirt lies on the floor where he fell, between the bed and a chest of drawers.

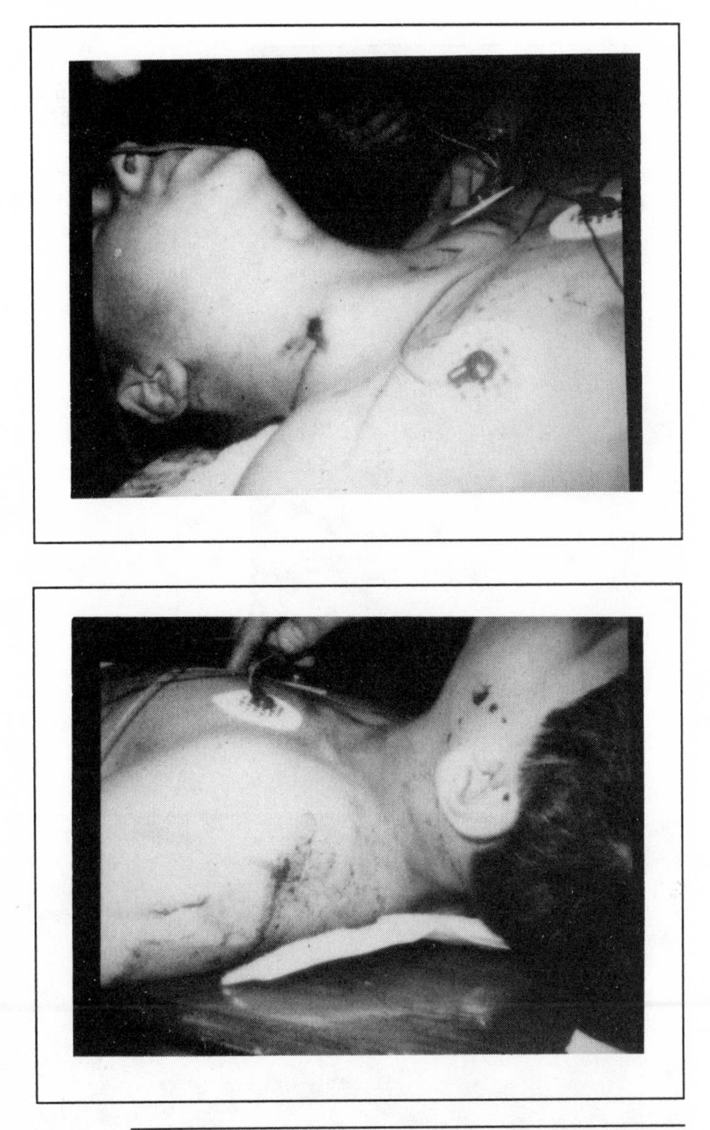

Lying on a back board and hooked up to monitors, Dwayne as seen in photographs taken by medical emergency crews. The top photo shows the entry wound in the right side of Dwayne's neck. The bottom photo shows the exit wound in his left shoulder.

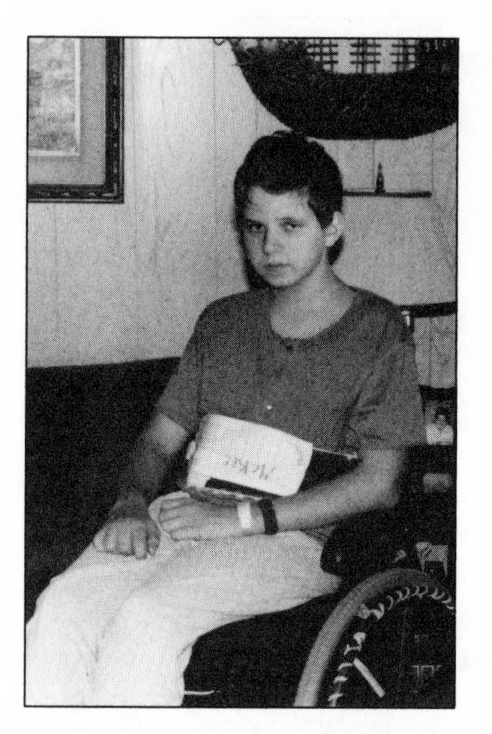

Left: Dwayne during his first visit home from the hospital, August 1985.

Below: Later the same year, back in the hospital. His mother, the author, is to the left.

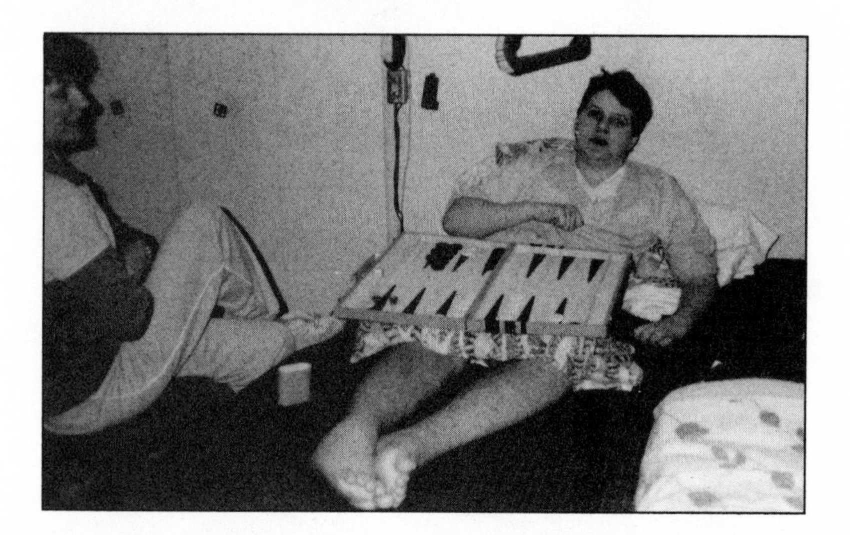

Dwayne McKee at one of his favorite pastimes, circa 1974 and 1990.

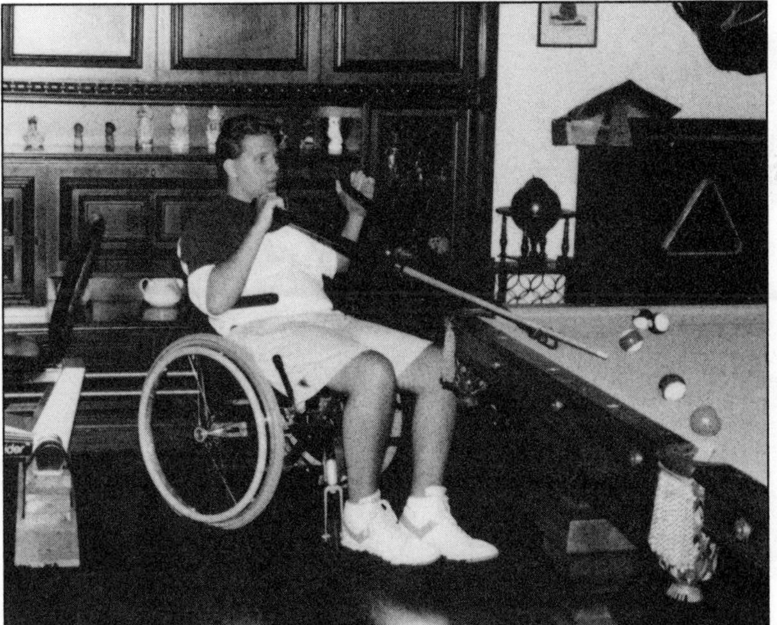

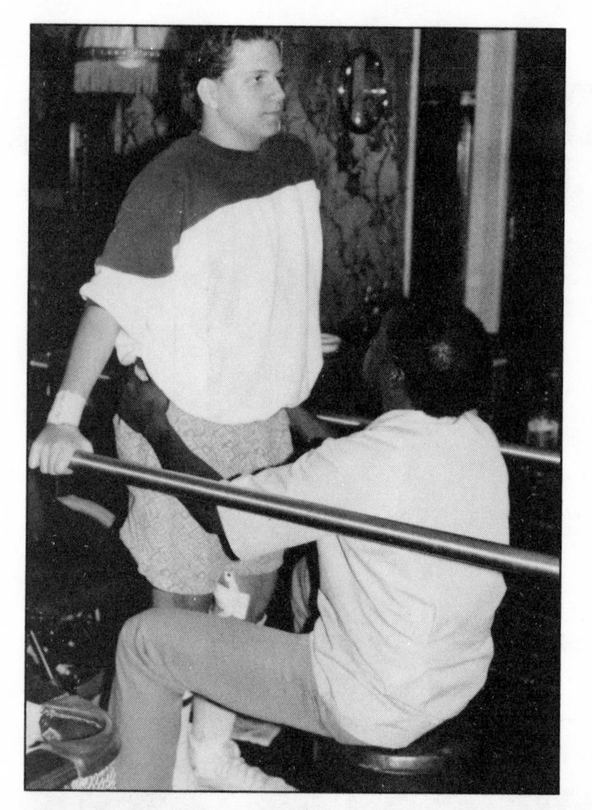

Left: Dwayne stands with the aid of parallel bars and his therapist, Willie Moch.

Below: The McKee Family: Mark and LaVonne, Gail and husband Jim, Dwayne, Kimberly, Deborah, Brian, and Carey.

Chapter XV

AT HOME

There was other anger, though it came from experiencing a world I had never previously understood. Dwayne took great pride in using a standard wheelchair. He had a way of working his palms together, then pushing the wheel awkwardly yet firmly so that he could propel himself wherever he desired.

A second wheelchair was motorized for Dwayne's convenience. He could travel for miles in that chair, having to stop only long enough either to recharge or to replace the battery. However, Dwayne tried to avoid the use of that chair if he could. It was a mechanical aid, the type of thing he had wanted to avoid since he was in rehab in the hospital. Unless he was so active with the rest of his body that he could view the chair as a vehicle for giving him the rest to enjoy his other activities, he resented being too weak to push himself.

Dwayne discovered that when we went to the mall, he could push himself if we could park close to the entrance. The short distance across the lot was not too tiring. Then he could maneuver through the mall on his own, a small touch of independence he treasured. However, his strength was finite, and the longer he rolled himself, the more tired he became. Eventually someone had to push him as he needed prolonged rest.

The handicapped parking spaces in large mall parking lots were ideal for Dwayne. The extra width of the spaces enabled him to use the van lift gate. We had purchased a used van, then modified it with a variety of straps to secure his wheelchair in place when he was driven somewhere. A lift gate had been added to the side door so he could roll onto a platform, then be raised or lowered as needed. If we did not use a handicapped space designed to accommodate his needs, then we had to park far from the entrance where there were two adjacent vacant spaces.

The distance was not great. A walk of moderate speed could cover the ground from where we parked to the mall entrance in two or three minutes at the most. Yet for Dwayne, his body shattered, the effort needed to control his arms to push the chair was far greater than the effort of an able-bodied person to walk, and the distance was exhausting. He could not push his own chair across the lot, into the mall, to the stores, and back. Yet he would not have anyone else push him. He was determined to learn independence. He had to cling to whatever shreds of mobility were left in order to feel right by himself. Yet each time the handicapped space was taken by an able-bodied person, each time the extra distance he traveled meant he had to rely upon the motorized chair, he was harshly reminded of his limitations, not his strengths. I hated the unthinking people who denied him what little self-respect he was able to generate because of their needless actions.

To the average person, there is no difference between a

wheelchair with a motor and one without. Most of us have seen both kinds, including the ones in some supermarkets that now offer electric riding carts for the disabled. They seem to be fun when we are tired. They remind you of the golf carts that are the preferred mode of transportation in retirement communities throughout the Southwest and in Florida. However, they are only enjoyable when you can get off them, stand, and walk. The difference between the powered chair and the one Dwayne moved with his hands was yet another difference between total dependence and moderate freedom. Each time some able-bodied person used the handicapped space, Dwayne's spirits sank. He knew he would be reminded once more of his weakness and his limitations.

The fight for dignity is far more difficult for the disabled than for anyone else. Catheters, waste bags, medication, special therapy, and other necessities are all reminders that you are almost less of a person. They are humiliating because they are a constant reminder of what is not rather than what is. To use the handicapped space, and thus to be able to enter the mall in a standard wheelchair, provided a sense of pride as fragile as Dwayne's body.

◆ ◆ ◆

When Dwayne returned home, we discovered that there was a special high school for handicapped students, another innovative service about which we would rather have remained naïve. The idea was to provide a fairly normal school environment to children who are physically unable to go to school. The class was held through a special telephone system. The hours were limited, from 8:00 A.M. to 1:00 P.M. with a break in between so that the students attending would be able to rest, have therapy, or do whatever else was a part of their day.

The range of students was great. One boy had multiple sclerosis, his limitations probably as great as Dwayne's. One girl had a badly broken leg, the result of a skiing accident, and would be forced to stay at home for several weeks. She would recover, though, unlike another girl who had juvenile onset leukemia, a disease that was likely to be ultimately fatal. Each student was incapable of attending regular school, lonely, and excited about reaching out to others with similar limitations.

The telephone system worked extremely well. We obtained a special telephone headset for Dwayne, and he delighted in sharing with the other students. The teacher's controls allowed him to work with the entire class or to mute all lines except the one of his choosing. That particular line was then used for a private conference with a confused student or one who was a verbal discipline problem.

The class was less inhibited than those in regular school, and if Dwayne made a friend, he would ask for the person's telephone number when the teacher was not talking. Eventually some of the students he came to know by telephone would visit him when they recovered from their injuries or illnesses. He even began dating one girl fairly intensely as a result of meeting her in the class, then having telephone dates for the three months it took her broken hip to heal.

Dwayne seemed to thrive in the special school. He would call the other students in the afternoon and evening, working out homework problems they all shared. It was as close to a normal life as he might be able to enjoy for a while, yet it was wonderful to see him make the calls. Socially, he was still trying to hide for the first few months. It was one thing for his friends to see him, to have a party for him, or to encounter him in the mall. It was quite another for him to consider throwing himself headlong into life as they were living it. He was not ready to learn if the friends would always accept him as he was or if they would gradually exclude him. They were young, strong, and mobile. Dwayne led much of his life in forced isolation. If he went to the beach, friends had to carry his chair across the sand. Someone else always had to drive. Somebody else always had to check to be certain restaurants, movie theaters, and other locations were wheelchair-accessible for him. It was impossible to know if Dwayne's limitations would be seen as an intolerable burden or just a minor inconvenience, the price they paid for the pleasure of his company.

◆ ◆ ◆

Just as we thought we were developing a routine of therapy, school, and recreation, we again learned the problems that can arise with unsupervised professionals. Dwayne wore a body jacket at times during his therapy sessions and while moving around the house. This was meant to stiffen his body, a physical restraint against the curvature caused by the spinal cord injury. It also made him slightly top-heavy and somewhat less mobile than usual.

Therapists are used to working with patients like Dwayne wearing body jackets, so that was not a concern. However, one afternoon, Carl Berin, the strapping blond therapist we were using, arrived annoyed. I don't know if he had difficulty with traffic, an argument with his wife, or what may have occurred. All that was obvious was that he was impatient and tense.

I sat on a bench in the room we had adapted for Dwayne's therapy sessions. Carl took the chair to move Dwayne. Then, for some reason never clear to either of us, he suddenly pushed Dwayne toward the wall.

The only way Dwayne could maneuver his chair was with the two palms of his hands. It was a slow, careful movement requiring great effort. Reacting to the unexpected was not something he could do quickly. Yet the only braking he could do was by grabbing the wheel, an impossible task at that instant.

The incident occurred so quickly, it was over before I could scream or rise to help him. Dwayne could not help himself, and in moments the chair smashed into the wall. The momentum knocked Dwayne so far backwards that the extra weight of the body jacket threw him severely off balance. His head hit the wall, and he tumbled onto the floor.

I gasped. Dwayne's neck might have been broken at that instant. What little movement he could make might have been shattered by the stupid temper of the therapist. All Carl could do was stare at Dwayne's fallen body.

"Please get him up," I cried.

Still the therapist did not move, and I knew I was not strong enough to lift Dwayne from that position.

I felt panic but would not yield. "I'll take the bottom of the wheelchair and Dwayne's legs. You pull him up from there!" I ordered. This time the therapist moved. Luckily, Dwayne's neck was not broken. In fact, he was not hurt at all. But we never again allowed Carl to touch our son.

◆ ◆ ◆

The wheelchair incident was the springboard for yet another ongoing problem we all faced: fear of the unknown, the unexpected.

In some ways, I was the quintessential mother hen, a worrier who wanted all her children to grow into independent adults, yet was secretly relieved each time they returned from bowling, shopping, movies, and dates. As long as they lived at home, I felt secure only when they were back under our roof. When they married, going their separate ways, I worried when they traveled or varied their new routines.

The worry was not obsessive. I did not telephone them several times a day to make certain they were all right. I just wanted their lives to be as happy and as trauma free as possible.

My concerns never kept me awake at night. They did not interfere with work or my relationship with Mark. I never tried to hold them back or censor their personal lives. They simply knew that they mattered to me, that their lives were important, that I cared. I did not fear my own death. I was comfortable with the idea that some day I would die first, hopefully never having to grieve over the loss of a child. My children were simply the best and most precious achievement of my life, and I loved them all dearly.

Dwayne had been like all the others before he was shot. But once he returned home from the hospital, I changed, and the incident with the therapist was just the first obvious sign of that change. My nights grew restless again. My days were spent fighting a desire to hover, to do everything for Dwayne, so there would be no chance of his getting hurt again. Fortunately, I knew that I dared not smother him with the worry born of a mother's love. Not only did I have to let him go, but I also had to encourage his doing so. Still, though I controlled my actions and the outward signs, inside I felt intense anxiety, and I only felt more relaxed when he traveled with another member of our immediate family.

However, what I thought would provide peace of mind ultimately proved not to do so. In his early days at home we purchased the van to make him more ambulatory and give him a sense of freedom. In it Kim drove Dwayne to the mall. Although Dwayne tended to call her a "lead foot," she was a safe, careful driver. But what neither she nor we realized was that securing a wheelchair to the back of a van is more complex than installing a seat belt. There are forces in all directions that can topple the chair one way while holding it fast another. We had installed special restraints, but we had not installed them to handle all the forces that can affect the chair while on the road.

One day while driving, Kim turned a corner at a speed that

was safe for passengers belted into the normal seats. However, it was too fast for Dwayne. As the van lurched sideways the belting design for securing his chair proved faulty. Dwayne's body weight shifted, making the chair unbalanced, and he fell on his side. This time he broke a bone.

Despite the fact that the accident was no one's fault, the incident was upsetting. Kimberly was badly shaken because she loved her brother and did not want him hurt.

Unfortunately, another problem soon joined the first and Kimberly was also driving the van when it occurred. This time, Kimberly was going straight through an intersection. The light was green and had been green long enough that there was no reason to slow down from the legal speed of thirty-five miles per hour at which she was driving. However, an elderly man had stopped in the middle of the intersection, facing the opposite direction in the appropriate lane for a left turn. He was at a complete stop, and Kimberly had the right-of-way. As Kimberly drove through the intersection, the elderly man suddenly turned left. Kimberly slammed on her brakes, but the crash that followed was unavoidable. Fortunately the other driver had just begun to accelerate and Kimberly was braking rapidly. But once more Dwayne was thrown from his chair, this time his body hurtling forward and onto the floor. Using techniques he had learned in physical therapy sessions, he managed to roll over at an angle where he could be more easily helped. However, he could not right himself or return to the chair. Luckily, two construction workers who had been working at a site near the accident rushed to the scene. They lifted Dwayne back into his chair and stayed with the kids until the police and an ambulance arrived. Once again Dwayne had broken bones, but he refused to ride with the paramedics. Instead, Kimberly telephoned me and I drove over in the family car, taking Dwayne to the hospital.

Both the physical and psychological effects of the two

accidents were traumatic. Dwayne had to stay at home to heal for several weeks. He could not continue working so intensely on his rehab program, and some of the skills so painfully gained were lost. Luckily, the loss was temporary.

It was from that second accident, as well as from experiencing flu and similar illnesses, that Dwayne learned how transitory his physical gains could be. The slide backward would be repeated each time he was too sick to keep his regular appointments with the therapists. Just a few days without working through his routine caused his body to weaken, and some of his motor skills became less precise. It was as though his body was a teasing seductress, providing pleasure one day, then taunting him with the memory of past delights while refusing to repeat the intimacy. He came to understand that every accomplishment could be countered by rapid deterioration caused by inactivity. The idea of "use it or lose it" is very real for a quadriplegic undergoing physical therapy. Although hard work would enable him to recover the skills he had learned, the repetition was frustrating, and we always wondered if there would come a time when loss of skills due to inactivity could not be overcome through renewed hard work.

As time went on I was harshly reminded of how fleeting life was, how little control I might have over anything that happened to my loved ones. I began to be plagued with recurring nightmares about the shooting. I awakened in a cold sweat, the dream as horrifyingly vivid as the first moment we entered the Townsends' bedroom and saw Dwayne's shattered body being secured by the paramedics.

I began to think I would never know a moment's true peace.

◆ ◆ ◆

As the days turned to weeks, the weeks to months and then a whole year, the progress Dwayne was *not* making became as obvious as his triumphs. I wanted Dwayne to be happy, and this meant in part seeing him do the things he enjoyed. For example, we had an antique billiards table in our home, and Dwayne had become an expert player growing up. Not being able to hold a cue stick was upsetting for him, and at first he did not want to consider adapting himself so that he could play to whatever degree might be possible for his body. Finally, with much encouragement, as frustrating for us as it was for him, he agreed to try.

Dwayne gradually learned that he had to adapt to his limitations, whether he wanted to do so or not. He had a device called a reacher that helped him hold things he could otherwise not grasp. It was a little like the pole-and-clasp device once used in general stores to reach canned goods on high shelves. The reacher would enable him to set the balls on the table once he got it balanced and under the control of the two fingers on his right hand that he could manipulate with some skill.

Dwayne also learned that he could not hold a cue stick and maneuver his chair into position. Instead, he would roll his chair into a position around the table from which he thought he could effectively make a desired shot. Then one of us would hand him the cue stick. He had to balance it, line it up, then find a way to push it so that it approximated the stroke he normally would have used standing, with two fully functional hands.

Nothing worked right at first. The stick would go to the wrong side of the ball or miss completely. There was no power to his play, the ball frequently lacking the momentum to do what he desired. Yet instead of feeling sorry for himself, he became determined to master the game again. He practiced for hours, his progress agonizingly slow. Yet eventually he was playing with enough competence to beat knowledgeable opponents who showed him no mercy.

I was so happy for Dwayne, so delighted that he could play a game that brought him pleasure. I was also thrilled to see him work with his baseball cards once more. He had loved his collection, loved mastering the names of the players, their statistics, and the growing value of the various cards. He understood the highs and lows of baseball cards as investment vehicles, knew the business, and saw his hobby as a future money maker.

Dwayne had thousands of cards and special protective holders to keep them from deteriorating. His hobby became a form of physical therapy as he learned how to grasp with the two reasonably functioning fingers of his right hand, then maneuver the rest of his body so he could organize them. He talked of one day opening a business buying and selling sports cards, and he convinced himself that he would be able to handle the challenge.

Again I was delighted.

Yet with all the pleasure, I also knew the truth. I did not care if Dwayne went into the collectible card business. Whatever made any of our children happy was fine with us. What troubled me was the idea that such a business might be the only thing he could do. Playing pool with a limited functioning body, using two fingers to maneuver his baseball cards, and being able to roll a wheelchair through a mall were not skills desired by employers. He could work in sales, perhaps doing an excellent job, yet when Mark and I had our stores over the years, we probably would not have taken a quadriplegic as a salesperson. We would have thought the image was wrong, that people would be uncomfortable, that he could not handle the work.

Now I knew better, understanding how effective Dwayne or someone like him could be. But I was not his future employers. I could not expect to sensitize them to the realities of the disabled. Even worse, I could not say with certainty how the customers would feel about someone with severe physical limitations.

Then there was the risk of illness. All quadriplegics have limited physical resistance. It is as though their immune systems have been damaged for life. If they are in the midst of people with colds, the flu, or some other contagious illness, it is almost a certainty that they will get sick. Would Dwayne have the maturity to work through those periods? Would he have the stamina? Or would he have to miss work just enough so he could not be placed in an important position?

As the enormity of Dwayne's loss struck me, I began to realize how much money it would take even to give him a chance. We did not have that kind of money. The only way I could think of to get it was to sue the people responsible for his condition so he could buy the tools that would assure him of having the greatest number of options possible in the job market. Then his future would not be limited to confinement in a nursing home or a spare room in the home of a family member. His limitations would be horrible compared with an able-bodied man, but they would be fewer than if he could not afford the aids he needed.

I began to focus on the lawsuit. As much as I wanted Jeff to know what life was like with the severe limitations he had imposed on our son, I wanted more to be certain that the Townsends' insurance reduced our worries about Dwayne's future. Money could not buy Dwayne's health. Money could not pay for what had happened. But money could pay for a companion, a different wheelchair, special exercise equipment as needed, the ongoing use of a rehabilitation specialist, a computer or other device to bring him into the business world.

Yet even this answer seemed beyond our reach. One afternoon, almost two years after the shooting, our attorneys came by the house. It had not been a good time. The damage to Dwayne's body, the slight curving of the spine, and the constant sitting had caused his right kidney to become slightly smaller than his left. Further checks revealed that Dwayne also had ongoing pain and swelling in his ankles, knees, left hip, and left leg. Numbness was constantly bothering him, and spasms were embarrassingly commonplace.

The money was critical. With the money, Dwayne's excellent mind could be supported. The value of his head would not be lost because of the problems with his body. Thus we eagerly met with the lawyers, hoping they would have good news about when Dwayne's case would go to court. They didn't.

We were horrified by what they told us. Bankruptcy laws in the United States are such that if we sued the Townsends, they could declare bankruptcy rather than pay us. They would be able to lead rich, full lives, keeping everything they earned after the bankruptcy. A judgment would be meaningless. The attorneys said they were going to drop the lawsuit. It was a non-issue.

Ironically they warned me that if I deliberately lied when writing my story, bankruptcy would *not* protect me from the libel laws. I would be faced with meeting a judgment even if I went to court. Damage a person's reputation in print and you will pay whatever the court decides, no matter how long it takes you to do so. Destroy a child's body, physically ruin him for life, and you can walk away without any responsibility.

That was what I was being told. That was what the American legal system had come to.

I looked at Dwayne, I looked at Mark, and I knew it was time to fight. No one had the right to do what they did to my son and not have to help him through the rest of his life. David Townsend had suddenly become not just the negligent father of a child whose actions so drastically changed my son's future, he had become a symbol for everything wrong with our laws and courts. I had to do whatever was necessary to be certain he paid. Then, with any luck at all, there would be a precedent that would allow others who had been deliberately hurt by the negligence of "fools" and had to suffer without recourse to have some hope.

Chapter XVI

RITES OF PASSAGE

No one talked with Dwayne about sex when he was in the hospital. The staff had special training sessions for other adult victims of spinal cord injuries, explaining what they could and could not do, as well as potential problems. A sex life is possible for a quadriplegic, although the couple may have to adapt to certain limitations. For example, while a male can sustain an erection, the sensitivity of the penis may be reduced to such a degree that prolonged stimulation is needed for him to achieve orgasm. Depending upon the partner's desires, this can mean a pleasurable prolonging of the experience, since the erection remains, or it may be physically irritating and emotionally unsatisfying. The stimulation may have to continue far longer than the partner desires such intimacy, at least several hours.

There were also penile implants for men who were totally unable to gain an erection. These implants allowed for a mechanical device that created an erection. The device could not increase the man's sensitivity or help him reach a climax, but it would allow him to satisfy a lover.

All of this was taught to adults. No one wanted to discuss sex with a child who had just entered the hormone-charged world of adolescence.

Dwayne had already gained some sexual knowledge before the shooting. He learned in the manner of most boys—from sneaked magazines and equally curious members of the opposite sex. There were the copies of *Playboy* he and his friends found in the trash or hidden away by an older brother, sister, or parent. Other experience came from the mutual "groping" of a willing partner, kissing and touching just enough to sense the mutual arousal. One girl had demanded that Dwayne French-kiss her. He had been just young enough to run away instead. As was usual with the onslaught of adolescence, though, he regretted his decision within weeks.

What Dwayne also did not know was that while many paraplegics and quadriplegics have a normal sex life, others do not. The mind is willing, but the body cannot respond. Or they become aroused, yet are unable to do what their partner desires.

By the night of the shooting, Dwayne had reached a maturation point where sex was intriguing to him. He had no idea what it all meant, but he did have feelings of physical desire, the ones that seem to be so much a part of male and female adolescence.

◆ ◆ ◆

As parents, Mark and I understood the potential problems for Dwayne. We worried about his future relationships. We worried about the possibility that either he would never have sex or the women in whom he was interested might be repulsed by his limitations. It was one thing to be unable to father a child. It was quite a different matter to be forced into a life of celibacy because of the actions of his best friend.

What we failed to realize was that sex for a man is mostly mental, and Dwayne's mind was primed and ready. Although he felt nothing in his groin area immediately after the shooting and could not have an erection while catheterized, he was keenly aware of the nurses who passed his view. He discovered that when he was propped at a certain angle, the light from the hall would backlight the nurses' uniforms. Their skirts became translucent and he was able to see their panties, the shape of their legs, and other details he found appealing. It was a little like looking at a partially covered centerfold. There was no physical response to his interest as he viewed the backlit nurses, but he pursued his voyeurism throughout his stay.

Once Dwayne returned home, the level of his fantasy sex stimulation diminished since he still had a tube inserted in his penis. It was several weeks before Dwayne began urinating in a controlled manner, allowing for the removal of the catheter. A few days later, Dwayne discovered that he could have an erection.

It happened when Karin, a young blond therapist, came to give Dwayne a massage. She was professionally trained, and her work was meant to ease his tense muscles. She was also a little on the wild side, delighting in teasing Dwayne when he asked about her more unusual cases.

"So you want to know about the interesting ones," she said in a throaty voice.

He nodded.

"Well . . . " she paused.

"Well?" he smiled.

"Well, there were times," she said, "when I was working on private patients that a man would offer me fifty dollars to stimulate him sexually. The man could not have intercourse for one reason or another, but he wanted the sensation that had been denied him." She leaned over Dwayne and began working on Dwayne's leg and groin area, playfully touching him just enough to stimulate him. She did not try to bring him to any sort of climax, because Dwayne's bedroom door was open and his parents were just down the hall.

There was also a surprising reaction on the part of the mother of a friend. The woman was married and had a daughter Dwayne's age. She was apparently seeking excitement outside of her marriage, and somehow Dwayne became a fantasy figure for her. She began telephoning him, making highly suggestive remarks. "You might say we were having telephone sex," Dwayne later commented, laughing about the incident. He did not know what she had in mind, nor did he really care. The situation was exciting his fantasies, at the same time reassuring him that he could lead a normal life.

Either Dwayne was too young to realize that the woman had emotional problems, or he did not care. She was no danger to him, and her telephone calls helped ease the frustrations of his daily routine. They also made him feel like a young stud, something any quadriplegic would enjoy.

Then there came a night when Dwayne and a couple of friends, including the girl's mother, went to a movie theater. They sat in the back in a location so dark that, even after their eyes adjusted to the low light, they could not see anything other than the screen. Dwayne was in his wheelchair, the others on regular seats, his friend's mother sitting next to him.

Suddenly Dwayne felt the woman's hand working its way to his crotch. She slowly and quietly unzipped his pants, stroking him to an erection, then playing with him. He was both shocked and intensely aroused. He thoroughly enjoyed the evening, though he stopped pursuing the relationship. A married woman was not someone with whom he wanted to be involved.

Later, as Dwayne's physical and emotional conditions improved, he began seeing girlfriends privately. By the time he was seventeen, this meant sometimes being in his bedroom for hours, the door closed as it usually was when he had friends—male and female—came to visit. We understood that going to the family room was often uncomfortable for him. With the door closed, Dwayne and his guest could watch television, listen to music, or talk loudly without disturbing the rest of us. I would see that they had refreshments, leaving them alone otherwise. Both Mark and I were delighted that he was not being abandoned by young people his own age.

Had Dwayne been fully able-bodied, we would not have tolerated dates that could so easily allow for sexual exploration. We would have been outraged if the parents of one of the boys Kimberly dated allowed the two of them to be in the boy's bedroom—whether or not the door was open. But we were convinced that Dwayne could not have sex and possibly never would. If he did become sexually able, we assumed we would know it, perhaps by his proudly telling us about the feeling just as he had shown off the first ability to move his toe and his arm. Thus we allowed Dwayne the privacy of his bedroom instead of insisting he stay in the family room or living room.

Probably, our ignorance was bliss. We did not know that Melissa, the girl Dwayne was seeing, liked him, was enjoying kissing him, fondling him, and being touched by him to whatever degree he could handle. Each time they were together, the relationship had become more intense. Melissa was a petite bodybuilder with long brown hair whose gym-sculpted figure was both flawless and arousing.

Finally, one night, everything was right. The limits they had set for themselves in the past were discarded. As Dwayne lay on his back, she moved closer. Her skirt was up to her waist, exposing a G-string panty. They were fumbling with each other's clothes, their faces flushed, their breathing intense, Melissa working to adapt her position to be most arousing for them both.

Not knowing of this, I chose that moment to knock on the door and to offer them refreshments. "Can I get you two anything?" I asked. I was thinking of sodas, some dip. I knew how much young people liked to eat when they got together, and I wanted Dwayne to know I cared about his friends' wants and needs. I was trying to be a good hostess, a loving mother.

Somehow Dwayne managed to sound almost normal. "Mom, please, we're just fine." He paused, reddening. "It would be nice if you went back down the hall to the family room."

I left happily, glad they were doing all right together. I had no idea I had interrupted their foreplay.

Unfortunately for Dwayne, the mood was broken. Startled, embarrassed, and a little afraid of what could have been the discovery of what they were doing, the two went no further. Before such a night could be repeated, the girl became involved with someone else.

Ultimately, Dwayne rediscovered his manhood with Sharon, a close friend recovering from a temporary injury. He met her through the tele-teaching program he was enrolled in. Their relationship developed over a three-month period when they talked by telephone almost daily after school was over. Through the mail they exchanged photographs so that when she was well enough to visit him, there would be no illusions on either part.

When that time came, they felt an immediate attraction. The dating progressed as it would have had Dwayne been able to walk, the only difference being that she had to drive them. Sharon had no concerns about Dwayne's limitations. She went to restaurants with him, to the movies, and to the beach at night. She had come to know him so well by telephone that his physical condition did not matter. She found him attractive, liked his sense of humor, liked *him*.

Eventually their relationship became more physical, the two as serious about each other as seventeen-year-olds can get. Good-night kisses gave way to dates where they deliberately went places where they could touch and kiss. Sometimes this was in the van or at the beach. At other times it was in Dwayne's room at home.

The couple was close, so close that I thought Dwayne might marry her. But neither was ready to consider such a step. They both had school to attend, and Dwayne needed to prepare himself to be as self-supporting as possible. They may or may not have been in love—neither was certain—but they were certainly in lust. The young woman wanted to be intimate with Dwayne, and she had no intention of waiting.

Then one night, when Mark and I were safely away, Sharon entered his room, closed his door, and ordered him to go from his chair onto his bed. She had come prepared with a condom. Dwayne was delighted by the way she made even protection from sexually transmitted disease and pregnancy a sensual experience unlike any he had previously known.

Neither Dwayne nor the young woman believed in one-time sex. They remained intimate until their lives changed and they drifted from being lovers to close friends. She began dating others, eventually marrying another youth.

When I found out he was seeing Sharon seriously, I was reluctant to talk with Dwayne. He and I had not discussed the girls he dated. As a result, when Sharon and Dwayne stopped seeing each other, I thought that the reason the two of them parted was because Sharon wanted a man "who could walk." In fact that was never a concern, and Dwayne has extremely pleasurable memories of their time together.

As a humorous aside, Dwayne discovered that one aspect of his quadriplegia enhanced their pleasure. His legs began to spasm uncontrollably during sex, a fact that increased the pleasurable physical sensations for them both. The memory is vivid and fills him with a mixture of delighted pride and amusement.

A week after Dwayne's reassuring rite of passage, I asked him, "Have you developed any sexual feelings?" My voice was quiet, a little shy. I did not want to embarrass Dwayne, since I knew having sex might always be impossible for him, and any sexual feelings might be but memories from before the shooting. Still, I could not help hoping that someday he could have a sexual relationship with a woman. Ideally, I hoped that I might one day have grandchildren from Dwayne. It was an aspect of life I did not want denied to either of us.

Dwayne looked at me, his face revealing nothing. Then he smiled that same old radiant smile and said, "Don't worry about it, Mom."

Chapter XVII

A GIFT OF PROPHESY

The happy moments lifted our spirits, but I still worried intensely about Dwayne's future, especially the money needed to provide for his education, physical therapy, and even his life.

I thought again about filing a lawsuit against the Townsends, but one set of lawyers had already called that hope impossible. I thought about other ways Mark and I could provide for Dwayne's future, but we were using all we had and more to provide for the present.

Then one day I was making a business call on Earl Hollings, one of our customers who was the owner of an appliance store in North Hollywood.

"How's Dwayne?" he asked.

"He has good and bad days," I said thoughtfully, "but the real problem is his future; it's very uncertain."

Earl scratched his chin. "Look, you may think I'm out of line, but one of my customers is Peter Hurkos."

"The psychic?" I asked.

"Yes," Earl nodded. "You might have heard of him because of his work with the police. According to rumor, he was a house painter, an immigrant from Germany or Holland. One day he fell off a ladder, and when he was revived he had psychic powers. A vision came to him about the Boston Strangler. He went to the police and many say he was instrumental in solving the case. Let me write down his address and telephone number for you."

That night I mentioned Hurkos to Mark. "I'm not sure I believe in such phenomena, but I don't disbelieve either," I said.

Mark was more skeptical but declared, "If you really want to, I'll go with you. I'll try anything to help Dwayne."

Although I had anticipated that making an appointment might be difficult, since Hurkos was often busy with the national media and other large performances, I was pleasantly surprised when his wife told us to come to their home the following Tuesday evening. She asked that we bring along some objects owned by the people about whom we wanted to talk.

Peter Hurkos's imposing home was in Studio City on a quiet tree-lined street leading up a winding hill. There were no sidewalks, so Mark parked our car next to a long set of steps intricately carved from stone around which were planted bright marigolds and other flowers. We walked up the steps and then down.

Hurkos answered the door. He was a formidable presence, though as I looked closer I saw a man of average height, a bit on the heavy side, with salt-and-pepper hair. As he reached his hands out to clasp mine, I noticed how very large and exquisitely formed they were. He led us into the living room of a home whose antique furnishings and heavy oil paintings seemed to have been transposed from another country, another era.

He looked as if he might be a professor at a prestigious Ivy League college as he directed us to the middle of the room and motioned that we should each sit on one of the armchairs flanking the sofa on which he himself sat down.

Then, in a thick accent, fingering the police photo of the shooting, some personal objects including a picture of Dwayne, and a key chain Jeff had given Dwayne in the early days of their friendship, Hurkos began to speak.

His thoughts seemed to filter from the present to the past and back again. At one point he said to Mark, "So you almost died once when you were seven or eight—almost drowned in a river." Mark gulped. It was true.

Changing subjects quickly, Hurkos said, "Dwayne . . . swimming will help him."

I smiled, "We were thinking of installing a special lift to help Dwayne get in and out of our swimming pool."

He nodded. "Goodt," he said, the accent pronounced again. He switched the key chain from left to right hand. "Jeff is sadistic," he suddenly announced. Mark and I looked at each other sadly. The information came too late to do our son any good. He continued talking about Jeff.

I interrupted. "Mr. Hurkos, Dwayne needs money to help him get the help he must have." I sat up on the edge of my chair. "We have been trying to sue the Townsends, but—"

"The lawyers say he has nothing you can touch," he finished the sentence. He leaned back and was silent a few moments. "Not true," he said, his voice rising, gathering fervor. "Not true. David Townsend has thirteen patents. His money is hidden in a Swiss bank located in the Bahamas." I bit my lip. Suddenly Hurkos picked up Dwayne's picture and, running his fingers up and down it, changed the subject. "Dwayne will have a sixty percent return to normal. He will stand. Probably he will need crutches, but he will walk."

I gasped, "If only it's true."

Hurkos stared at me with intense dark eyes. "Wait, you will see."

As we were leaving, Hurkos mentioned that he knew an attorney in Beverly Hills who specialized in personal injury cases. He suggested we call David Glickman to get his opinion about our case and gave us his address and telephone number.

Going home in the car, we spoke of nothing but Hurkos. Could what he said have any credibility? Should we believe him? We decided to take his advice to wait and see but to phone the attorney he mentioned immediately.

I called Glickman the next morning and to our delight was given an appointment that afternoon. We only had some of the paperwork concerning our previous attempt at a lawsuit when we went to see David. Immediately upon meeting him, however, we felt there was something very comforting about the man. He was large, over six feet tall and at least 220 pounds. His suit was neither fancy nor cut from cloth that implied great wealth. It was the type of suit worn by a lawyer who did not want the jury to think he was profiting at the expense of his clients. And while his clothing was probably more expensive than that worn by David Townsend, the impression was one of a regular person, someone who might be your neighbor getting ready for church, not a high-powered attorney who had won million-dollar judgments.

Even Glickman's watch seemed simple, far better than a Timex yet appearing to be the type that might be carried by a small jewelry store. We later learned that it was worth a thousand dollars, and the watch he wore when not on the job was a Rolex probably worth more than we spent on our car. Obviously, he was a success, and since he took a percentage of his clients' settlements, meeting his expenses from that sum, his triumphs were his clients' triumphs.

Although we badly wanted him to take our case, we were honest with him about all the reasons we had heard the case would result in a probable loss.

Glickman spoke of why he had entered the law, his philosophy, his passion for justice. As to the other lawyers' opinions, Glickman said in a forceful tone, "I disagree. I feel that there might be a legal situation where the Townsends or their insurance company might be financially liable." He met our eyes directly and spoke with feeling. "I am interested in taking on the case."

We nodded. Since his fee was contingent upon our winning, we had nothing to lose. We signed an agreement to have him represent us.

As we talked after leaving his office, Mark and I discovered that both of us had the same favorable reaction to David Glickman. It was more than outward trappings of success that impressed us. David Glickman seemed to genuinely care about us and our plight. I didn't feel as though he saw us as another case, a chance to pit his skills against those of the attorneys for the insurance company. He wasn't playing the macho games of teenage boys as some lawyers seem to do. His concern was not so much winning as achieving justice—an important difference. He wanted what was right for Dwayne under the circumstances of the case we had brought to him. He did not want to hurt anyone. He just wanted the results of our effort to be fair, and we felt as though he was the first person in a position to help who thought that way.

While Glickman would work for a percentage of what was won, our bills continued to mount. Mark and I had to take out a home equity loan to meet the ongoing medical and therapy expenses. We also installed the pool lift, then hired Abbie Thorndike, a recreational therapist who worked for the Northridge Medical Center. We knew Abbie and so were not worried about her care of Dwayne. She worked with him in the pool as I watched, trying to learn as much as possible. It was in the pool where more of his muscles could be stretched and exercised, including those of his hands.

We also installed parallel bars, then after conferring with Abbie, who felt Dwayne needed someone stronger and heavier to work with him, we hired a male therapist that she recommended. Dwayne was growing more fully into manhood; his body was taller and heavier than in the past. The parallel bars would allow him to experiment with standing erect, but his condition also meant that he would be likely to fall with regularity.

The man we hired was named Willie Moch, and all of us immediately liked him. He was a well-trained, skilled, and caring black man. At nearly two hundred pounds with the build of an athlete, he also had the strength to handle any problem Dwayne might have.

The system we purchased was a simple one. The bars were extremely strong yet designed to be assembled and disassembled quickly. Their height was adjustable, and we found that they could best be used in our living room. We would set them up near the pool table when Dwayne had therapy, then take them down afterwards so we could play pool.

It took several sessions with Dwayne before Willie was willing to try to have Dwayne stand. First, he needed to stretch the muscles of Dwayne's legs and feet. This he did through the range of motion exercises that had been done, in one form or another, since Dwayne had been shot. The difference was that this ranging was more extreme, as Willie was trying to build Dwayne's strength and flexibility. Even if Dwayne could not control them, the muscles still needed the strength to support his body. Since he had been sitting or laying down for years, this meant preparing him in ways similar to what an athlete might do when about to attempt an unfamiliar event. The workouts became more complex, preparing the muscles for what they would have to endure.

Finally Willie said, "Dwayne is ready." I was not so sure. Dwayne, confined to the wheelchair, was able to be mobile. He knew how to maneuver his chair, how to handle it safely. Trying to stand meant new concerns. What if his legs buckled and, in falling, he broke his neck? What if he struck his head? Broke his arms? The possibilities were numerous and frightening.

Did Dwayne really need to learn to stand when he could not walk? Was the potential of this therapy greater than the risks? I told myself that I had to trust. I had to let Dwayne do what he felt was best, what Willie believed would be most beneficial.

Fortunately, Willie was as cautious as I was nervous. First, he performed the range of motion exercises with Dwayne's legs and feet. These were like warming-up exercises, meant to relax Dwayne's body and prepare the muscles for the stress they would have to endure.

Next, Willie attached strong plastic braces to support Dwayne's calves and feet, covering them with oversized tennis shoes with the toe portion removed to make room for the plastic. The wheelchair was placed behind Dwayne, the wheels secured so it would not roll. If Dwayne fell backwards, he would go only a short distance before landing on the chair. Willie then used a combination of a Velcro strap and his own legs to support Dwayne's left leg, the weaker of the two. Finally Dwayne managed to raise his arms and rest them on the twelve-foot-long parallel bars.

Dwayne began pushing. He pressed against the bars, trying to exert enough pressure to raise himself. The effort appeared to be as intense as that of an able-bodied person attempting to lift the front end of a small car. His face grew red, sweat appeared on his forehead, and his shoulders strained against the bars.

There would only be one try that day and we all knew it. It made his attempt harder to watch. His actions were like those of a weight lifter trying to smoothly lift the heaviest weight of his career. Any pause in the effort would cause muscle fatigue so great that the weight would crash to the floor. Only through continuous effort would he succeed.

There was absolute silence in the room. I realized only when I felt myself suffocating that I was holding my breath. Slowly I exhaled, still staring at Dwayne.

Dwayne's body vibrated slightly, the muscles rebelling at the effort. Still he rose, not by inches but by centimeters. He was moving slowly, steadily.

And then he was doing it. Dwayne was standing erect! There were braces on his feet and ankles. Willie's legs served as a block in front to prevent Dwayne's collapse. The chair served as a block in back. Dwayne's balance was precarious, and it was obvious that he would fall at any moment. But for those precious few seconds, Dwayne was standing! It was the first time in more than two years.

I wept with joy, tears streaming down the sides of my face. I didn't know if I was witnessing the beginning of a dramatic change in Dwayne's abilities or the end. Maybe he would never be able to do more than stand in the manner he had just accomplished. Maybe this was to be the first of many achievements. It did not matter. Our son had just discovered that with hard work the seemingly impossible could be achieved. If the lesson he learned at that moment was the last he learned, he would be a success. Perhaps he would never have much use of his body, but he would have the mental determination to succeed. An able-bodied person who does not know he can triumph over seemingly insurmountable odds will always be "handicapped," as opposed to the one who understands that far more is possible than the "experts" know.

Dwayne dropped back onto the chair, exhausted. He was like a runner who had reached what he thought was the maximum of endurance, then gone a mile beyond. He had used his body to its fullest, and he was joyful even as he knew he had to rest.

Reinforcement was critical if Dwayne was to strengthen his body enough so that the ability to stand was more than a one-time experience. Willie came three times a week, and each time, after Dwayne's other workout, the effort was repeated. There would be the range of motion, the bracing, and then the exertion to stand.

I had watched his awkward attempts at walking when he was a baby. First he had to learn to stand erect, usually using a wall or a table to support himself. Then he began the slow, rather jerky gait so common to all babies when they must consciously readjust their balance with every step. Sometimes he fell. Sometimes he made it across the room, perhaps walking from Mark to me and back again. Yet each time he became smoother and steadier.

The baby steps became baby runs, his knees pumping high, his movements a parody of an athlete's, yet always improving. Soon there was no stopping him, whether on foot, on his tricycle, on his first two-wheeler. He was a boy on the go, and the progression from those first awkward steps to walking was a steady one.

But not during those sessions with Willie. After the first time, because of Peter Hurkos's words or my own thoughts, I may have had fantasies of Dwayne trying a step or two, then a walk the length of the parallel bars, and then tentative efforts without support. I expected him to repeat the experience of his toddler years. I expected him to quickly become a young man with full physical abilities.

The truth was that Dwayne had been shot. The scar from the bullet wound had healed and slowly begun to fade a little. A casual observer would probably miss the mark or assume it was a blemish from birth. It was in Dwayne's attempts to stand that the reminder of the shooting came back; a horror so disgusting that it at once attracts and repels. I could see no more advances after the first time, just a repetition of the same action. Three times a week he stood. Three times a week his face reddened, the perspiration soaking his forehead, his muscles becoming fatigued from the exertion. Always he achieved his goal. Always the goal remained the same. I could see no other improvement.

Chapter XVIII

"GUNS GUNS GUNS!"

It was July 1988 when Dwayne became a television star of sorts. NBC News was producing a special on the violence caused by the ownership of handguns in America. Connie Chung was the star, discussing the fact that there are two thousand times more deaths by handguns in the United States than in England, Canada, and other areas of the world. The special was meant to show the way violence has permeated the nation, from major cities to small towns. It showed how easy it is to obtain handguns and how many handguns there are in the United States.

The producers of the program wanted to condemn handgun ownership and perhaps the ownership of all guns.

Mark and I thought that such an idea was overreaction. We

feel it is not the guns themselves—whether handguns, rifles, or shotguns—but their misuse that is dangerous. We respect target and competition shooters. We feel people who hunt and follow the law are not criminals, nor are those who own handguns for protection.

We do feel there need to be stringent controls. Background checks should be made to be certain someone does not have a criminal record or psychiatric history where they could use a weapon violently. I support the Brady Bill, which requires a waiting period before the purchase of a handgun. After all, there is no reason that someone can't wait seven days unless they are acting on impulse, in which case if the person can buy the gun too easily, someone might die.

Not long after we hired David Glickman, a producer for the NBC special called "Guns Guns Guns!" telephoned him after learning about our case. David called us, and we agreed to spend a day being interviewed and videotaped. The producer of the segment did a preliminary interview, then introduced us to the reporter, Maria Shriver, the niece of the late President John Kennedy.

We wanted to discuss the safe storage of handguns, and we stressed it during the approximately forty-five minutes that Mark and I talked with Maria Shriver on camera. Ms. Shriver also talked with Kimberly, and, of course, she and the crew spent extensive time with Dwayne.

We thought the program was going to focus on Dwayne. However, when the program was aired they showed victims in high-income, predominantly white communities such as Winnetka, Illinois, where the average family earns $95,000 and 13,000 people live in relative luxury. And they showed low-income black victims of drive-by shootings in the ghetto. What is happening to children in middle-class neighborhoods was only touched upon. Dwayne was profiled because of the unusual nature of his shooting. The longest segment was of a black prison inmate who had used a handgun in committing a violent crime. We were disappointed that our segment had been cut to perhaps three minutes of the hour-long show, and it heavily downplayed the tragedy.

In reality, there was an intense struggle each time Dwayne went in and out of the van, all of which the camera crew taped. Yet it was edited to a close-up of Dwayne's few good fingers using the switches to maneuver the lift.

Another few seconds showed Dwayne eating a sandwich, seemingly with ease. If you knew what to look for, you would see one hand curled under the other and used as a prop. They did not show the difficulties he had getting to the point where he moved the sandwich to his mouth. Dwayne spilled nearly every sandwich he tried to eat because of his awkward maneuvering. It was as though he had to remake it repeatedly before he reached a balance by which he could maneuver the sandwich to his mouth. Yet it was only the last of his efforts that was shown, the time when he finally was in control, the eating a fairly smooth action.

There were also a few seconds of Dwayne playing a slow game of Ping-Pong. He had developed enough grip with his working fingers to hold the paddle. His arm movements were limited, yet he had a degree of skill of which we were all proud.

Yet we wished the producers had shown him working out during a therapy session. It would have been much more revealing of his limitations and daily struggles.

There was one nice part of the interview. Maria Shriver gave us tickets to her husband's closed premier showing of his new movie, *Red Heat*, which was being previewed at the Academy of Motion Picture Arts and Sciences in Beverly Hills. A closed-off section in the middle-rear was reserved for us so Dwayne's chair could be comfortably positioned.

Ironically, the movie was filled with violence, bodies

seemingly flying everywhere as the result of the thousands of rounds of ammunition fired in the movie.

Eventually, the video footage from all the interviews conducted in four different regions of the country were further edited and the final results were aired on television on July 5, 1988. It was shown at 10:00 P.M. in California. Mark, who had been adamant about the safe, responsible handling and ownership of handguns, had all his remarks edited out. My appearance was limited to one quote that I suppose was meant to touch a universal nerve with the viewers. I explained that I had always been afraid of Dwayne getting hurt when he was out riding on his bicycle. I said I never expected that he would be shot by a handgun.

Later we would hear comments about the show from friends, acquaintances, and strangers we frequently saw in supermarkets and elsewhere.

However, in our own lives we were living with the tragedy every day. It was in this period that Dwayne and his friends started going out more often. He liked to claim that having people look at him did not bother him, but it was obvious by the way he held himself, the comments he made, and the flare-ups of stomach acid that it bothered him very much. Eventually, though, he seemed to accept the reality. He talked of liking the curious children when he finally realized that their stares and questions were without malice.

As time went on Dwayne began wearing shorts again, though this was not until he no longer wore the drainage bag. He found that it was more fun to go to the beach, even with friends having to carry him on his chair to wherever they were playing, than to stay back because he couldn't wheel himself across the sand. He also started going to clubs where there was dancing, moving on the dance floor with the other young people.

Perhaps part of Dwayne's success on the dance floor is the result of the way kids dance today. When Mark and I were young, kids held each other while they danced. Today it is as though the kids are dancing by themselves. Watching them, it is sometimes impossible to tell who is dancing with whom. Having a wheelchair rolling about in the midst of bodies gyrating does not seem out of place in such a scene. Some of the girls danced with Dwayne by gyrating their bodies as he moved back and forth. Others danced around him, and to his delight, occasionally one of the girls would sit on his lap, moving her upper body while Dwayne maneuvered the chair.

Still, even while he was engaged in activities that others his age enjoyed, there were subtle problems for him. Some of the kids liked to take snapshots of each other and their activities. Our family had always taken pictures of everyone, especially during Thanksgiving and Christmas. Now Dwayne hated the picture taking, thoroughly embarrassed by being "trapped" in his chair. In addition, when we first resumed the picture taking, the click of the camera's shutter caused Dwayne to flinch. The sound reminded him of the cocking of the revolver hammer the day he was shot.

Despite the ongoing problems caused by his injuries, in the summer of 1988 Dwayne's life seemed to be moving forward. He was still standing three times a week, and now he was helped by a new Swedish Keen Cage Brace that would lock his left knee in place. His left side was substantially weaker than his right, the side the therapist had previously had to brace with his own legs and the Velcro strap.

Dwayne completed the high school courses he had taken by telephone that summer and got his diploma. Afterward, he enrolled in Pierce College for the fall term. Kimberly was also attending the same school that September, and she planned her course schedule to match her brother's when possible. "I'll be able to help you with your books and any other needs since the college is not fully equipped for wheelchair access," she said proudly.

We were proud, too. Yet we also saw mounting bills of proportions we had never anticipated. Most of the creditors were understanding. We paid the people who had to be paid first, including Dwayne's therapists. We delayed purchases of all but necessities. And Mark handled the maintenance of our home and business vehicles as much as possible.

It was obvious to us that money determined the quality of Dwayne's life. And we could not help but see that money probably would determine the length of Dwayne's life, as well.

Early in the recovery stage we used to joke about the cost of items Dwayne needed. It seemed that each piece of equipment was one thousand dollars. It cost a thousand dollars for a simple wheel chair. It cost a thousand dollars for a piece of exercise equipment. It was as though the manufacturers of aids for the severely disabled had all gotten together and decided that a thousand dollars was the perfect price for every item they sold. Their bookkeeping was simplified, and the dealers would only need to vary the local sales tax when they made sales.

As the weeks turned into months and the months turned into years, the jokes were forgotten. Almost every parent thinks of their child as priceless, but we learned because of the shooting and its aftermath that our son had a price, and unless we could find a way to meet it, he would die before his time. Even worse, he would die without achieving whatever his potential might be.

The only hope was David Glickman's effort with the lawsuit. Yet we had been warned that such a lawsuit was hopeless; that was the reason our other lawyers backed out. We could only pray that our new attorney was doing more than trying to humor us by pursuing a hopeless cause.

Chapter XIX

TOO LITTLE, TOO LATE

We soon learned that David Glickman was quite serious. In October 1988, the Townsends' attorneys arranged for a spinal cord specialist to come from San Francisco to check Dwayne's condition. It had taken more than three years for the family to show any interest in how Dwayne was doing, and now it was their lawyers who wanted to know. Even worse, the lawyers were hoping that the truth was a good deal less serious than we were saying. Ideally, Dwayne was faking, perhaps able to walk, to juggle, to race over hill and dale on his bicycle. At worst, perhaps there had been so much recovery that the damages would be slight. Whatever the case, the doctor they sent was considered so knowledgeable that whatever he said could be believed.

There were other experts seeing Dwayne as well, including a nurse whose specialty was the long-term care of spinal cord patients. She knew the costs that would be incurred, and it was her job to estimate for the court how much money would be necessary to sustain Dwayne until age seventy.

Finally, new depositions were taken for the case. Dwayne was interviewed, along with Jeff Townsend, his parents, and five board members from Anafuel, the corporation David Townsend headed. The corporation was to become a key factor in Glickman's handling of the case.

Mark and I had very mixed feelings as the case escalated and David Glickman moved into high gear. We are proud people who believe in hard work, self-reliance, and caring for our family. We feel that we must be responsible for our own actions, and that if we face hardships in life, we must work to rise beyond them.

Going to court to try and receive payment from the Townsends was an action we did not consider immediately after Dwayne was shot. There was intense anger. There was a desire to see Jeff Townsend punished. There was also a desire for the Townsend family to acknowledge both responsibility and concern. But had the family acted differently, perhaps the impending court date would never have occurred.

We wanted the Townsends to show some genuine concern for Dwayne, to say they were sorry, to reach out and try to help. We were certain that the Townsends were insured with at least a standard home owner's policy that would pay for accidents in the home. We would have settled for whatever that meant, a figure we later learned was a maximum of one million dollars. Even had the amount been substantially lower, we still would have accepted it.

Instead, there had been no words of compassion, not even an "I'm sorry about your son." There had been the telephone calls, the hospital visit, the incident with Kimberly, and others. Some events were known to be directly connected. Others seemed likely only because no one else had reason to do what had taken place.

There had also been no effort on the part of the Townsends to meet any financial responsibility. Our previous lawyers had gone so far as to say that any effort to collect assets could result in a personal bankruptcy, absolving the Townsends of financial responsibility.

We felt overwhelmed with emotion. Our son had been denied the basics of human kindness and decency. Someone had to stand up for his rights. Someone had to challenge people who refused to act in a proper manner. Now with David Glickman spearheading the attack, we could not help but feel it was time to make the Townsends pay for what their son had done to Dwayne.

David Townsend's Anafuel Corporation allowed for a gasoline-naphtha-alcohol mixture that greatly improved car mileage. As Townsend explained when Glickman deposed him in June, "Naphtha is 55 octane when it is first refined in a refinery. You can't burn 55-octane gasoline.

"So we bought naphtha at a discount price because it is less than the cost of gasoline, mixed alcohols with it, which was the cheapest form of raising the octane, and raised the octane to 92 and sold it as gasoline."

David further told our Glickman, "When Anafuel first started, we were the ones who changed most rules of the California Air Quality Management District on alcohol-based fuels. Up to that point they allowed gasohol, but no other form. We proved to them, because of all the testing that we did, that methyl alcohol mixed with phenyl alcohol in the presence of [*unintelligible*] created good octane and met their standards. It reduced the unburned hydrocarbons and carbon monoxides, and it was a better gasoline in California."

He claimed that it was in use for a number of municipal government car fleets. Townsend legitimately held patents, but David

Glickman explained that the holding of a patent does not mean that the claims made for the product are valid. And David Townsend was making millions of dollars through the corporation.

Insurance for the Anafuel Corporation was provided by a company called National Union. Townsend had stated when questioned by Glickman that the National Union insurance policy, which was for ten million dollars, "covered the gasoline terminal as well as all the properties owned by Anafuel." The terminals were where the chemicals were stored. But among the properties owned by Anafuel was the home in which the Townsends lived. David Glickman felt that this policy, as well as at least one other he was able to uncover, would protect us. He felt the negligence of the Townsends in leaving the loaded gun available to Jeff related directly to the insurance for Anafuel because of the mingling of all assets. Glickman contended that Anafuel and the Townsends were one and the same. But the difficult job would be proving it.

To get this proof, Glickman decided to question people employed by the corporation who might be privy to information about David Townsend's use of corporate funds. He hit several dead ends, but in January 1989 he got lucky.

When deposed, Nancy Harris, the corporate secretary/treasurer who also owned five thousand shares of stock, stated that she thought David Townsend mismanaged the funds of the corporation. When Glickman questioned her, she said: "Money was removed from the company by check and given to various doctors, attorneys for this case, the McKee situation, and for defense of the son, Jeffrey, in Juvenile Court in Sylmar."

Harris said that after the shooting, she discovered that the Townsends' home had been purchased in the name of Anafuel Corporation. She said that it was then that she was shown "an insurance policy and other documents, copy of note, deed of trust and some other note, too, I think, the prior owner concerning their case. They were presenting documents they had hidden in a closet in the flooring. She [Marilyn Townsend] showed me the insurance policy."

Nancy Harris further explained the document's location: "There was a—what do you call it—a little safe in the floor in the front hall closet that you removed a board and pull out a box, and in that box was what I perceived was the copy of the deed of trust, recorded deed of trust, the note, some other papers which she didn't bother to open and some kind of hazard policy that they had on the house, liability, whatever, general coverage. And I noticed that the Anafuel name was on it."

In questioning David Townsend, Glickman also wanted to clarify the issue of who had given Townsend the gun used in the shooting and whether it was a personal or corporate gift. Present were Attorney Kevin J. Stack, representing David Townsend, and Attorney Keith Walden, representing Anafuel.

Glickman began:

Q: Now how did the gun get presented to you and what was said at the time of its presentation?

A: There were some presents that the family had brought and other people had brought in, and Crockett presented it to me and said it was from the Board of Directors to me, and it was a .38 Smith and Wesson snub nose. They said it was for my protection for the house, since I had had a break-in. They didn't want the president of the company killed.

Q: You were the one who knew the biggest password of all?

A: Yes.

Q: If you had died—

A: They would have been in trouble.

Q: What would they have done?

A: They would have had problems getting in the computer to find out anything.

Q: Did the board know you were the only one who knew the key password?

A: Yes. Everybody knew it. They all had access to different parts of it, so they would probably be able to get all the information out a bit at a time, each of them getting their own information out.

There were very few things, except the patents themselves, that would have been in there that they couldn't have gotten out, but there were copies at the house.

Q: It would have been quite an involved process?

A: It would have been quite an involved process.

Q: So were they concerned not only about your safety, but the safety of the contents of the home?

Objection. Lack of foundation.

Q: [Mr. Glickman, continuing] When they gave you this gun, did they say that?

A: No.

Q: They said they don't want you killed; they wanted you to have some protection.

A: Yes. It was because we had the break-in and it was a pretty scary thing.

Q: The board knew of this?

A: Yes.

Q: Why was it so scary?

A: It was two o'clock in the morning. Everybody was asleep. I am a very light sleeper, and I heard something that sounded like the sliding door. So I got up and came downstairs and the house was dark. One of them hit me when I came through the room. I got up and fought back, and that is the reason they left.

They could have just as easily shot me. I didn't even think anybody broke in. I thought it was one of the kids. The last thing I thought of was two guys breaking into my house. It was kind of a shock.

Q: Did you put a burglar alarm system in?

A: We had one. I don't know how they got past that. It was on.

Q: It was on?

A: They came through the door and the alarm didn't go off.

Q: I think you had some long guns at the house?

A: I have had those for quite a while.

Q: You didn't have access to those at the time of the break-in?

A: Yes. If I knew somebody was breaking in, I could have got the key and unlocked the cabinet and got it out.

Q: Why is it you kept the long guns locked with the keys you just mentioned and not this pistol?

A: If it hadn't been for the break-in, the pistol would have been locked up in the gun cabinet.

The reason I kept it in the bedroom in the cabinet was because of that break-in. If it had been another two, three months later, I would have put it back in the gun cabinet.

Q: You kept the pistol loaded?

A: Yes.

Q: Unlocked?

A: Yes.

Q: It was not supposed to be locked up at the time of this shooting?

A: No. I didn't know my son knew where it was. I didn't know anybody else except my wife and I knew where the pistol was.

◆ ◆ ◆

Later Glickman talked to David Crockett, who was the member of the corporation board who had given Townsend the gun.

The gun was originally bought for personal use. Crockett had been a Green Beret in the military, and he purchased the revolver after moving to California to work for Anafuel. He said, "Mr. Ray Arsnow, an associate in the company that I was working with before, had known Mr. Townsend for a number of years prior to my ever meeting any of those folks. And he's the type of person that believes in brown-nosing his boss.

"And he says, 'Guys, we got to get David—we have to get David a nice birthday gift.'

"Well, Bob Pronier was kind of against that, and I was, too, but I had the gun, and Ray said, 'David likes guns. He's got about a dozen of them of his own in his home now,' which there was a big gun case there, as you walk in the door, and there all these guns was.

"And he had an old .38 which was rusty. I wouldn't have shot it, I wouldn't have given it to an enemy of mine to shoot. So we decided collectively, the three of us, would give him that pistol that I had bought for myself. And I said, 'Each one of you give me sixty-five dollars apiece, because the gun cost about two hundred dollars. And here's the gun. Give me your money.'

"They give me the money, cash. I put it in my pocket. We went to his home. Ray Arsnow gave him the gun and said, 'Happy Birthday.'"

Crockett explained why he was comfortable giving the weapon as a gift. He said, "Back in 1982, when I was—when it was hinted to me that I might be in charge of security, and that I might be going to California, I wrote the State of California on their handgun laws, and I corresponded with them. And I knew legally that I was being covered by us giving him that gun and that we were not infringing or breaking any law. Therefore, I did go along with it. And at the time, I was a little short of money, and I gladly let them talk me into going along with giving him that pistol for his birthday, so I could have their $130, because I needed the money." He also made it clear that the gun was not a gift from the board of directors.

What was most interesting to us was when our attorney asked Crockett about the story concerning an intruder in the Townsend home that same year. His reply was that he didn't remember anything about a break-in, though he would not swear that it never happened.

Since the time of the first trial, David Townsend had moved his business to Texas. He claimed he moved from six thousand to ten thousand boxes of records there, opening Anafuel in that state, using the California Corporate Charter which had been suspended in 1986 by the Secretary of State for nonpayment of franchise tax fees. Glickman explained that when he requested those records in order to have the documents necessary to prove who really owned the Townsend home, David Townsend said, "They're in Texas locked up by the landlord because Anafuel didn't pay it's rent there."

What the other lawyers had failed to see and what Glickman now felt was clear was that the Townsend family had essentially made Anafuel their lives. The business and personal existence of the family was so intertwined as to be the same.

◆ ◆ ◆

On a warm day very like the day of the shooting, David Glickman began his opening statements in Los Angeles County Court. He alleged that the corporation held the title to the Townsends' house. In addition, "the corporation's mainframe computer, which cost $106,000, was as large as the size of a desk, was an IBM, contained three hundred million bits of information, and was kept at the Candlewood residence.

"At the office they did have a small computer, according to testimony, but it did not have a printer, and you could not input or extract data at the office. That could only be done at the corporate residence, and only David Townsend knew the magic password to get into all aspects of the computer.

"That becomes important, because he testified and will testify that he was given the gun in question by the board of directors because the board did not want the president killed because only he knew the magic password to get into the computer and get all of the data out.

"All of the trade secrets of Anafuel were kept only at the Candlewood residence. By that I mean all of the records of the accounts payable, receivable, all the checks that were written were only found at the Candlewood residence. That's where the patent was kept.

"And at all times no less than two and sometimes up to fifty drums of the secret additive that Anafuel made—its reason for existence—there was always at least two fifty-five-gallon drums of the secret at the residence.

"All the board meetings except for one were held at the Anafuel residence. David Townsend worked three to four hours each night at the residence on Anafuel, and he called to and from its refinery in Ojai on a nightly basis on corporate affairs.

"I think the court will find that everything between David Townsend and Anafuel were so intertwined that its separateness, if any, is transparent to non-existent.

"That's why alter ego is an important doctrine in this case."

I sighed, remembering that the concept of alter ego, as David Glickman explained it, meant basically that a business and executive—in this case David Townsend and Anafuel—were so intertwined that the corporate checkbook was as likely to be used for buying new underwear and food as it was for purchasing office supplies. There was a closed corporation of thirty-five people. There was a board of directors, but no corporate minutes were ever kept. It appeared that Townsend also spent corporate money to arrange for the purchase of his house without the awareness or approval of his board of directors.

Whenever someone plays fast and loose with the assets of the corporation, he risks becoming, in effect, one and the same as the corporation. Glickman felt that in this case, that meant that the corporation and its insurance company could be held liable for what took place in David Townsend's home and by members of his family. Since businesses and business insurance policies usually have far more assets than an individual, forcing a pay-off without fear of bankruptcy is possible.

In the courtroom, Glickman's passionate voice rose.

"Speaking of alter ego, the evidence will show that David Townsend and his wife, Marilyn Townsend, used the corporate funds as their own. By that I mean there will be evidence that they paid their household expenses, food, groceries, beauty parlors, anything they wanted by using Anafuel corporate checks.

"In fact, when David Townsend moved Anafuel to Texas, he bought a house there in his name using an Anafuel check, and he paid mortgages using Anafuel checks. I have the proof of that because we subpoenaed the lender's files.

"The Townsends bought cars for their children and even their children's wives using Anafuel checks. They paid their son's legal defense for the shooting, approximately fifteen to twenty thousand dollars, by using Anafuel corporate checks for their own personal use and for the use of their son.

"And they drew salary when the other employees went without paychecks from Anafuel."

As our attorney had told us, according to the concept of alter ego, David Townsend's negligence in the keeping of the handgun used to shoot Dwayne became Anafuel's negligence. The insurance company for Anafuel was responsible for negligence on the property owned by the corporation—the Townsend home.

David Townsend's business had been run in such a way as to benefit his family at the expense of investors and creditors. We were told that he was a confidence man, that he used his corporation to defraud others. Only as we sat in court did we realize what we were up against. It was almost possible to have compassion for

Jeff, knowing what his father was like.

Though I was ready to stare him down, David Townsend was unfortunately not scheduled to take the stand that morning. He "had the flu" and was unable to appear in court. He also did not appear on Tuesday, January 16, 1990, so at 3:00 P.M., Judge Robert Letteau cryptically commented, "Tell me the sad tale of woe. What happened to Mr. Townsend?"

His lawyer, Kevin Stack, responded, "Your Honor, we did get a request for Mr. Townsend to be available for 1:30 this afternoon. Everything was squared away, and I had spoken to him yesterday, and that was fine.

"I did get a message this morning—I was in a deposition—that he was ill with the flu but that he was going to leave at one o'clock and would still try to come.

"When I was done with the deposition, I checked back at his house and received word that he had gone to the doctor at eleven o'clock and was still going to try to come as far as the son knew. I did put a call also to the work, and as far as they knew, he wasn't there, and he was going to the doctor and was planning on being here.

"I have checked periodically and there's been no further word at the home or at work, and their understanding was that he was going to the doctor and was going to be here. I only imagine he's taken more ill than at first he thought he was going to be."

The judge was also told that Marilyn Townsend was in Columbus, Indiana, with her mother, who allegedly had an accident.

Having listened to these excuses, the judge indicated that testimony was to continue.

David Glickman further explained, "The Townsends stripped out the money of the company for their own personal use and benefit, like for paying for beauty parlors, groceries, cars for the Townsend kids and their wives, and pantyhose, and all that sort of thing, and then also the Townsends paid for Jeffrey's criminal defense, the juvenile proceedings, with corporate funds."

Our attorney continued, "All that stripped the corporation to such an extent of its corporate treasury that it never filed tax returns, and never paid its franchise fees, and the Secretary of State suspended the company in 1986."

The next morning David Townsend still had not shown. We all felt it was obvious that he was faking illness. One of the witnesses, John Cejka, a long-time friend of David Townsend and former head of research and development for Anafuel, talked with the attorney for Townsend just before court began again. He told the attorney, Charles Carpenter, that he had had dinner with David the previous evening at a restaurant called The Darby.

The call to Cejka had been at approximately 8:00 P.M. the previous day. However, Kevin Stack, the other attorney involved with the defense in the case, explained to the judge his knowledge of what happened.

"When I checked in later in the day at the Townsend household, they still had not heard back from the dad. I finally received word around seven o'clock from Jeff that the dad had arrived back at home, that he had been at a Dr. London at the West Hills Medical Center with the flu. He had 103-degree fever. He had been vomiting during the day and had worsened since he left the message with the office, which prompted David Townsend to go to the doctor. He said that Mr. Townsend had gone to sleep and was just not feeling well at all with the flu."

David Townsend telephoned Stack around ten o'clock that evening. The attorney said, "The doctor had told him it was a thirty-six-hour flu, that if by some miracle he felt better in the morning he would come along with Jeff."

Stack explained to the judge that he had called David Townsend that morning after talking with his fellow attorney. He told David about the comment by Cejka. "And all I can say is he adamantly denies it and says he has not seen Cejka for a couple of days and it's entirely not true."

As the case continued we heard one of Dwayne's doctors testify concerning Dwayne's future. We were glad Dwayne wasn't there to hear him. He did not think there was anything about his damaged body that he did not already know.

The physician who testified was an expert on spinal cord injuries such as Dwayne's. He had worked with hundreds of patients, and he was familiar with the medical literature concerning thousands of others. He was an expert on the long-term experiences of both full and partial quadriplegics. What he had to say shattered my emotions so thoroughly that I cannot talk about it without a catch in my voice.

He said a quadriplegic can never feel comfortable with existing body strength. A healthy person who achieves top physical conditioning is able to maintain his or her body through regular workouts. Strong muscles remain strong if exercised. Powerful normal lungs retain their capacity for breathing if maintained through aerobic conditioning. But all quadriplegics, no matter how well exercised, may lose some or all of the strength and abilities they have gained, literally overnight.

We already knew that when Dwayne worked on the parallel bars, missing even one therapy session made repeating an exercise almost impossible. When this happened he had to learn a skill all over again. He was like a baby who, having learned to crawl and then to walk, would have to go back to crawling if he or she stopped walking for twenty-four hours.

We believed that Dwayne's sex life was going to be healthy and normal when he began having intercourse. The doctor showed that quite the contrary could be true. There easily could come a time when he would lose the ability to have or sustain an erection. Dwayne could find himself unable to satisfy both a woman and himself.

Even if Dwayne could always sustain an erection and enjoy

intercourse, his sperm count might diminish to the point where he could not impregnate his wife. Or he might find that he could no longer ejaculate sperm. Even worse, if he and his future wife wanted a child through artificial insemination with his sperm, viable sperm might have to be taken through a surgical procedure. Instead of his being able to masturbate into a sterile container, an invasive surgery currently costing between $15,000 and $20,000 might be needed.

The doctor said all of Dwayne's organs were overtaxed just from his being in the wheelchair. Under all *normal* circumstances, Dwayne's heart and lungs would have to work far harder than if he was not in the wheelchair. This situation was not unique to him. It was a normal situation for all quadriplegics. It was also the reason that they needed to be exercised as much as possible. The heavy burden on vital organs often cut their lives short.

Dwayne's kidneys were not in their normal position because of the chair. Kidneys only remain healthy when someone is standing and normally active. Endless sitting is destructive for many people. Thus his kidneys might stay fine or they might deteriorate. It would not be unusual to have him experience kidney failure or severe damage. A kidney might have to be removed. He might have to go on a dialysis machine. He might die. . . .

There were other problems as well. There was the risk of blood clots. There were concerns about the potential for bed sores becoming infected.

As always, the doctor stressed the fact that Dwayne was more likely to get worse than to get better or even to stay the same. The exercise and the physical therapy might improve his health to assure he could better resist illness. But his resistance would always be less than that of a fully able-bodied individual. Even with the exercise, he could lose strength, lose what little mobility he had. Dwayne might lead a full, productive life. Dwayne might also find himself deteriorating so rapidly that nothing could keep him out of an extended-care facility. Instead of seeing Dwayne's current abilities as something he would enjoy his entire life, they might be the high point of his existence following the shooting. All the money, all the therapy, and all the hard work might prove to be useless in keeping him alive. Both the quality of his life and the quantity of his years might be drastically reduced.

The money would enable Dwayne to fight. Yet just the fact that he was a quadriplegic might mean there was no hope. The bullet might have been his death sentence, the execution taking years instead of seconds.

The doctor's testimony about Dwayne's future so unnerved us that we were almost glad to turn back to the subject of Anafuel. Still, I sighed heavily as the parade of witnesses continued. We were familiar with the depositions of the men and women connected with Anafuel whose testimony would be heard. We were prepared for the general way in which David Glickman would be establishing a claim to insurance payments. We were ready for our day in court in every way except the one that claimed our attention on January 17.

There was nothing that could be done to ease the shock of hearing the opening of a courthouse elevator door followed by the whispered comment "That looks like Jeff Townsend."

Although I had been nervous during the first days of the trial, I had not thought too intensely about Jeff. It was only when I heard his name that I panicked.

I whirled around and stared. My stomach felt as if I was on one of those high-rise building express elevators when it rapidly drops from the top floor to the basement parking garage. So many emotions overwhelmed me—anger, fear, hatred, disgust. There was even nausea, as though I had suddenly been exposed to the odor of a sealed room filled with fresh vomit and excrement.

Then I was no longer in the hall of the Superior Court of Los Angeles. I was at home, hearing the telephone at 6:40 P.M. on

June 7 all those years before.

I remembered the feelings if not the words. Answering happily, my voice reflecting the pleasure of the evening Mark and I were going to enjoy.

Then Jeff's voice, devoid of any real emotion, telling me that Dwayne had been shot.

The room. I remembered the room. I looked at the elevator and saw the bedroom of the Townsend home. I looked at the passing attorneys, the people arriving for jury duty, security personnel, reporters covering one or another of the trials, yet all I saw was the bedroom where my son was lying on the floor, blood pumping from the wound in his neck.

I heard nothing, felt nothing, saw nothing except what had occurred then. It was as though Jeff Townsend was the conductor of a voyage through time, a human transporter to a mother's worst nightmare. He had robbed my son of a normal life. Now he was controlling my awareness, my memories. One glance at his features—slightly older, fuller, his body taller, his back straight, his gait smooth, graceful, as Dwayne's would have been, *should* have been—and the courtroom seemed momentarily to vanish.

I don't know how long I stood there living the horrors of the past. Five seconds? Ten seconds? It could not have been more than that, though in the midst of the experience, I thought it was without beginning and without end. The vividness of the momentary memory might as well have been on an endless loop of Technicolor movie film into which I had been inserted for all eternity. Then, as if the flashback had never happened, I suddenly became aware once again of being in the courthouse. Jeff walked past us without a comment or even a glance. There was no arrogance. There was no effort to avoid my eyes. He simply passed us as you or I might pass a stranger on a crowded street. He walked to the end of the hall, looking out the windows, waiting as we were for the trial to begin.

Then I noticed Jeff's clothing. He was wearing Levi's, a T-shirt, and tennis shoes. Everything was clean and casual, the type of outfit that told the world, "I'm just on my way to school. No big deal. Nothing important happening today. Just one of those things you've got to do sometimes."

Tears of anger came to my eyes. Jeff and Dwayne were close to the same age and probably would have been close to the same size had Dwayne's body been able to grow naturally.

Dwayne could not stand tall and straight as Jeff could.

Jeff could walk into the shower before court. Dwayne had to roll in.

Jeff could put on his Levi's, slip on a pair of socks, put on a pair of shoes. Dwayne couldn't do any of those things. Showers were time-consuming and frustrating. Putting on clothing was an excruciatingly slow process without assistance, yet to ask for help would be to give in to more of the paralysis than he dared. No matter what his physical limitations, his emotions required him to achieve whatever was possible, no matter how long it took.

But Jeff knew none of that. Jeff could walk into the elevator, and if he was in a hurry, he could run up the steps. Jeff could walk down the hall, walk into the courtroom, and walk to the witness stand.

I had to fight back more tears watching him. Jeff Townsend acted as if he was going to a class at school. There was no sense of respecting either the court or the reason we had all gathered there. There was no hint of remorse. There was no sense of the magnitude of the impact his action in picking up that handgun and pulling the trigger had caused.

Had Dwayne been killed, there would have been a small degree of healing possible, although the loss would have stayed with us all of our lives. The pain would have been a constant ache, a prolonged agony caused by an emptiness in my heart.

But Dwayne's survival meant ongoing anger. No matter how

much he achieved in life, I'd always wonder if he couldn't have accomplished more or gained that success sooner without his limitations. Each time I saw him struggle to stand erect or watched him work to shift his body from the wheelchair to the bed, I hated the person who so senselessly destroyed what should have been. Dwayne's struggle was a constant reminder of the shattered dreams of the past and the uncertainty of the future. And Jeff Townsend was the cause of all the pain.

◆ ◆ ◆

It was originally David Townsend, not his son, who was supposed to testify first. I had not really thought about Jeff's presence; I suppose I was more prepared for the father.

Not that I thought that David Townsend was innocent. Although the court had ruled negligence in the shooting of Dwayne, I felt that Jeff had deliberately pulled the trigger. I felt that in so much as a young teenager can understand a deliberate act of murder, Jeff had tried to kill my son. I hated him for that, hated that he had never suffered for his crime.

Jeff had also been the person who telephoned us to tell us about Dwayne. It was Jeff's voice I remembered from that night when Dwayne was shot.

Yet the truth was that David Townsend had been the person who gave his son the opportunity to shoot Dwayne. I don't know if the boys would have gone up to the elder Townsends' bedroom had the parents been home as we expected. I don't know if Jeff would have left the gun alone had his father been present. All that was certain was that there was no reason for Jeff to have access to a loaded handgun. He was too young, untrained in safety, and not a responsible enough individual to have such a weapon available. At the very least, the gun should have had a trigger guard. Ideally, it should have been stripped of the bullets, the weapon and the ammunition separately stored in locked drawers or a locked cabinet.

Despite all that, seeing and hearing David Townsend testify would not have been quite so upsetting for me. My anger was focused on Jeff, the person who pulled the trigger, whose life had once been so intricately interwoven with my son's.

Now I was inside the courtroom. I watched as Jeff Townsend's name was called. The case did not involve him. To me he looked as though he had not a care in the world. We were interrupting his day, of course, but other than that, the trial did not interfere with his life.

Chapter XX

JEFF AND HIS FATHER

As Jeff walked to the witness stand, I glared at him, my hand gripping Mark's. I had no idea what I wanted from Jeff. A confession? An apology? To be strapped to the chair and electrocuted? I couldn't stand the sight of him, yet I couldn't keep my eyes off him.

Jeff never looked at me, though. I might as well not have existed.

The clerk droned, "Raise your right hand. Do you solemnly swear that the testimony you may give in the cause now pending before this court shall be the truth, the whole truth and nothing but the truth, so help you God?"

Jeff, looking straight ahead, said, "I do."

"Be seated," the clerk said.

"State and spell your name, please."

Jeff, his voice clear and strong, said, "Jeffrey, J-e-f-f-r-e-y, Lee Townsend, T-o-w-n-s-e-n-d."

When David Glickman asked about Marilyn Townsend, Jeff said she was in Columbus, Indiana, though she called him each night. The judge interrupted the questioning to say, "Mr. Townsend, will you advise your mother that we're not going to be able to wait for her—this isn't like a restaurant—until the end of the month."

There were also questions about Jeff's father. Jeff said that though David had stomach flu, he could be there that afternoon. When questioned about the dinner with John Cejka, Jeff said he knew nothing about it, that his father had not been home for dinner the previous evening, though he presumed his father was at the hospital. Jeff did know of The Darby Coffee Shop, which was on Sherman Way in Canoga Park, but he didn't know if that was where his father had eaten. However, he said his father was looking better and would be present in court that afternoon.

Then came questions about the day of the shooting. Again Jeff said that the shooting was an accident. He told of the gun being his father's birthday gift, received on May 5. He explained that the gun was kept loaded and unlocked in his parents' bedroom dresser. He said that both parents were aware of how the gun was kept.

David Glickman began showing Jeff police photographs of the shooting scene, having Jeff confirm that each one was from that time and represented a different aspect of what occurred. It was all simple, straightforward, mostly "yes" answers confirming what was obvious in the pictures. Yet my reaction was hostile. I felt as though everything he was saying was a lie. I tried to keep my face a blank, though I suspect my expression conveyed my hostility.

My stomach clenched as our attorney asked questions related to the shooting, pointing out to Jeff each time his story changed from his original deposition—such as when Jeff said on the stand that his father specifically told him not to use the guns in the house, then David showed that he had said something different in his earlier deposition.

Jeff's testimony mostly went over material covered in the earlier trial. Always Jeff stressed that it was an accident, though the details differed from the earlier statement.

During a break in the questioning, Jeff went down the hall, nonchalantly moving to a distant location so he would not have to acknowledge our presence. He was eighteen, almost six years older than when he had told our son it was time to die. He had grown into manhood, adapting to his changing body, his movements smooth and strong, the perfection of youth. Dwayne had also grown into manhood, adapting to his changing body, being propped with pillows, declaring triumph when he could be braced enough to stand erect, his movements slow, awkward, so limited that I wanted to weep each time I watched him try for a little further reach, a little greater dexterity, a little more muscle strength.

I wanted to grab Jeff, to shake him, to slam him against the wall and ask him why he had done this to our son. Why did he do it? *Why?*

I tried to control myself. I held Mark's hand so tightly that the skin turned white from the pressure, the form of my fingers lingering briefly on his flesh. I fought back the tears, not wanting anyone to confuse the frustration of overwhelming anger with tears of sadness. I had shed far too many of those since the shooting.

When Jeff finished his testimony, it was time to break for lunch. The judge arranged for Jeff and a deputy sheriff to call his father to remind him that he was to be in court that afternoon at 1:30.

Security was tighter in Judge Letteau's court that afternoon, though I thought little about it at first. David Townsend arrived, and while I was angry, most of my emotions had been spent when I looked at Jeff that morning. A constant churning nausea remained. It would have been a good day to bake bread, though I think I would have preferred David and Jeff Townsend's heads to be substituted for the raw dough. I could picture myself kneading their flesh, then turning them a quarter turn, grabbing at their flesh, and twisting, pounding, pulverizing some more. Instead, I sat, watched, and listened to David Townsend's testimony, never realizing how that day would end.

Glickman first established that David Townsend had deeded his residence, the home where Dwayne was shot, to himself and his wife, Marilyn, on May 5, 1987. He claimed that the authorization came from the board of directors of Anafuel, which had met in Texas approximately six months earlier. He also stated that when the house was first purchased in the name of Anafuel, there had also been a board meeting.

David Townsend then explained that he personally owned 55 percent of the Anafuel stock, his wife and four oldest sons owning an additional 20 percent. Only Jeff, the youngest boy, was without a share. The remaining 25 percent was divided among thirty-five stockholders. Under California law, more then thirty-six total stockholders would have resulted in a situation requiring the close legal scrutiny that he wanted to avoid. I would have thought that the number of family members would have meant that the stock was divided among forty-one people, but apparently this was not the case. Instead, the family members were considered a group of one because of the close, direct relationship.

Much of the questioning was designed to show that the house in which the Townsends lived had the mortgage in Anafuel's name. According to the testimony, Townsend had given a $45,000 check to Anafuel, which had, in exchange, provided the same amount of money to Home Federal Savings for the mortgage.

Each piece of evidence had to be painstakingly established before a new one was added and built upon. Our attorney had to establish the fact that the money spent by the corporation and the money spent by the Townsends was often the same. He had to show that when the family was negligent, it was the same as the corporation being negligent. Otherwise, the insurance company would not be liable.

As the questioning continued, David Glickman began showing how Townsend had lied about many aspects of the business. Perhaps the biggest lie had to do with the computer, an issue that would come up repeatedly since it was apparently the heart of the operation, the keeper of the formulas for his additive.

Glickman's attention was riveted on Townsend as if they were the only two people in the courtroom.

Q: Did Anafuel have a mainframe computer kept at the Candlewood residence?

A: No. It had a computer kept at Candlewood. It wasn't Anafuel's computer. It was my computer. But we used a lot of Anafuel's tapes and a lot of the records there.

COURT (i.e., the judge): What kind of a computer?

WITNESS: IBM.

COURT: What model?

WITNESS: It was—the one at the house was Xerox. IBM compatible.

By Mr. Glickman:

Q: What you call a mainframe computer?

A: No.

Q: Was there ever a mainframe computer at the Candlewood residence?

A: We referred to it as a mainframe, but it really wasn't a mainframe computer. I still don't know very much about computers, so my terminology is probably pretty wrong. I know how to call up information, but I don't know how to store it.

Q: You don't know how to store things?

A: I don't know how to operate that.

David Glickman then asked Townsend about the purchase which he said was made from Argos Automation in Los Angeles.

COURT: How much did you pay for it, approximately?

WITNESS: Two thousand dollars.

COURT: And you paid for that personally?

WITNESS: Yes.

COURT: Were you reimbursed for that by the corporation?

WITNESS: No, I was not.

GLICKMAN: If I could just have a moment, Your Honor.

COURT: Did that two thousand dollars include the peripheral equipment, the printer, the hard drive, if any, as well as the monitor?

WITNESS: Yes. It was the complete set.

COURT: Did it have a hard drive?

WITNESS: Yes, it did.

David Townsend explained that there were in fact two computers. There was an IBM that his son, Randy Scott, had purchased when he was going to college. There was also a Xerox computer, the one that cost two thousand dollars including all the accessories. Townsend explained that the Xerox had a hard drive of 40 megabytes and, with the monitor, was about the size of a bread box.

Q: And would you call that computer that Anafuel had at the house or you had at the house a mainframe computer?

A: I may have referred to it in there like that because I didn't know anything about it.

COURT: On page 28, the question by Mr. Glickman:

"What size would be the computer that you had at the

house?"

"Answer," your answer, Mr. Townsend:

"About the size of a desk. About three hundred million bytes of information. It was pretty good size."

"Question: What did the computer, that computer cost?"

"Answer: About $106,000."

"Question: It's what you call a mainframe computer?"

"Answer: That was the mainframe."

"Question: That was kept at the house?"

"Answer: Yes. It wasn't all purchased at one time. We had added onto it all the time."

WITNESS: We had both computers put in there together. My son's as well. But it didn't belong to the company.

COURT: What didn't belong to the company, the IBM?

WITNESS: None at the house.

COURT: What are you referencing when you talk about three hundred million bytes of information and a computer cost of about $106,000?

WITNESS: I have no idea. I didn't know anything about it until I started checking into it after the deposition.

COURT: You thought this two thousand dollar computer might have cost $106,000?

WITNESS: I was considering everything at the office and at the house. Everything.

Suddenly it began making sense to us. David Townsend was talking about a "main computer center" at his house that consisted of his computer, his son's computer, and a laser printer. For the first time we started to understand that David Townsend had not just blended corporation and family into one entity, which formed our basis for challenging the failure to pay insurance after the shooting. It seemed clear to us that David Townsend was a liar, a con man, someone who was as dishonest as he was reprehensible.

We waited to see what else was going to be discussed, but the judge had other plans for David Townsend. He ordered a short break, with court to continue again at 3:20 that afternoon. Then Judge Letteau announced that an order was to be prepared to assure that Townsend would be available first thing in the morning. The bailiff said, "There's a phone call about that right now, Your Honor." And that was when two armed officers who had been waiting on the sidelines moved in.

They arrested David Townsend. When he was testifying with contradictory statements about his $2,000/$106,000 computer, about records that were in Texas unless they were in California, about all manner of things that ultimately made little sense, he had been calm, relaxed, seeming to me to be a seasoned liar who never became rattled. Each time he was caught in a lie, he changed his story just enough so that the next statement might sound plausible. He was a gifted story teller, but suddenly things changed.

Silver handcuffs glinted in the light as they came out. Steel bands snapped on his wrists, keeping them close together, constricting his movement.

I saw one of the officers saying something, reading David Townsend his rights, I presumed, but I heard nothing. I was in shock—surprised, but delighted. Though not understanding exactly what was taking place, I was enjoying the humiliation, the limitation, the fact that someone else was willing to force David Townsend to be accountable for his actions.

The cuffs were on Townsend only briefly while there was a search of his clothing and possessions. He had been accused of committing crimes in Texas. He had apparently left that state to avoid facing the charges. He could be extradited, yet he apparently felt that the safest action he could take would be to hide in plain sight in the courtroom. By finally showing up to testify, he seemed to think that no one would check his record to see if there were any outstanding warrants for his arrest. But Judge Letteau, his staff, and others involved with the case had done just that.

Townsend had been accused of being a confidence man in Texas. His new type of gasoline might be a concept that would actually work, but his business practices were cited as intensely dishonest. He had apparently been selling more shares in his business than actually existed. He seemed to be walking the fine edge of a tightrope that ran through his interlocking businesses. One false step and his sources of income could be revealed as having been achieved through dishonest means. I did not know how his actions, and the warrant, had been discovered. Although we were not the type of people who had ever reveled in others' troubles, seeing that man humiliated made us feel wonderful. Later we were told he would be facing up to seven years in jail—not the life sentence Jeff had given Dwayne, but a shattering future for someone who came to the trial a wealthy businessman and who was now accused of being a self-confident criminal.

Judge Letteau kept a straight face during actions that must have amused him. After the shock of seeing Townsend arrested, something that the judge had helped arrange, the processing seemed to be taking an unusually long time. The judge looked over at us and commented that David Townsend was probably selling phony stock to the deputies who were handling the arrest procedure.

Finally the judge faced Townsend. He knew that Jeff's father had been avoiding the civil and criminal charges brought against him in Texas. So far as we knew, he had fled that state to avoid the arrest that had just taken place. Yet the judge did not accuse him of such an action. He just said:

"I know Mr. Townsend wants to address these legal issues, whether they emanate in Texas or otherwise. There are obviously a number of procedural matters that have to be dealt with by the sheriff's office.

"There's a bus leaving for downtown now. It's not the last bus of the day. The concern is if he's not processed today, he may not be available tomorrow morning or perhaps not even at any time tomorrow.

"I don't want to break at this time, but I think under the circumstances we should make every effort to see to it that Mr. Townsend has the opportunity to take this bus that's waiting and deal with those issues so we have him back here as early as possible tomorrow."

The clerk of courts and the judge arranged for David Townsend to be placed in custody to assure his appearance at the proceedings. The warrant for his arrest from Texas was such that it might be possible for him to post bail and leave. It might be possible for him to avoid coming to the courthouse in the morning. But by also placing him in custody with the sheriff's department relative to our case in which he had to testify, the judge could prevent Townsend from being able to escape. "That's no bail," said the judge forcefully.

David Townsend's arrest did nothing to help Dwayne, but it still made us feel better. It was as though someone had finally recognized who the victim was. Jeff had never been made to pay for his crime. The insurance company had avoided its responsibility. And David Townsend had conducted business as usual. Now we learned that the "business" was apparently corrupt, that he was allegedly a con man who had cheated many people, and Judge Letteau was finally beginning a procedure whereby justice might be rendered.

Later that night when Mark and I talked about the arrest, we each seemed to remember it in our own way, best suited for our own peace of mind. For example, I remember David being taken out, searched, stripped of his clothing and being forced to wear the colorful jumpsuit that was standard jail issue. To me, that was the most humiliating experience David Townsend could endure at that moment.

Mark, filled with an anger he had been unable to fully resolve during those agonizing years, remembered even greater humiliation. He remembered David Townsend being arrested even earlier that afternoon, then having to testify while in handcuffs. As he recalls that day, Townsend stood for an hour or more, his wrists secured in a way that made escape impossible, and having to testify in a manner that made him look like a physically dangerous criminal.

Mark needed a memory of vengeance. I needed the reassurance that the court believed us when we said how dangerous the Townsends were, how seemingly amoral Jeff and his father could be. We each remembered the events of that afternoon based on our inner needs for healing.

The next morning, David Townsend did not show up for court, though this time the judge knew exactly where he was. Townsend alleged he was having a heart attack, though a physical examination failed to reveal any problems. Perhaps he was having chest pains due to anxiety. Perhaps he was faking. Whatever the case, he was in court that afternoon, wearing the colorful jumpsuit that is assigned to all criminals staying in the jail. It was yet another embarrassment for him and, I have to admit, a pleasant one to witness.

Our attorney began pressuring Townsend about the computer he kept at home. It was an important issue, because it further established the close link between the family and the corporation. While many people have home offices, it was Glickman's contention that the Anafuel Corporation and David Townsend were one entity, and that the board was a rubber stamp; the corporate money was used as family money. The computer being at the home instead of the official office was another factor. Since by then Townsend was changing his statement from his earlier deposition, one or the other statement had to be a lie.

David Townsend's earlier deposition said that the computer's memory and full printing facilities were at the house, only a terminal allowing information review being at the office. In court he said that a full computer existed elsewhere.

Townsend said that he couldn't remember if Nancy Harris came to the house each week to enter the payroll in the Anafuel/Townsend computer. Then our attorney read Townsend's original deposition, in which he said that she faithfully was at the house using the computer to handle the $14,000-per-week payroll. Townsend had also said in the earlier statement that all accounts receivable and payable were done at the house.

Jeff's father admitted that each section of information related to the Anafuel operations had a code word known by only one person in addition to himself. He alone knew how to get into every file. However, again there was controversy. In court he said the procedure was involved. In his original deposition, he said that a single password would get him into all the programs. Whatever the truth, watching him constantly try to explain away his discrepancies, the irony was the code word he had used. By typing this word into the computer, he could do anything he wanted with the Anafuel records.

That code word was—"LOVE."

Other information about the house was brought out. At least two fifty-five-gallon drums of the company's main product ingredient, which he called X-1A, were kept at the house. Should there ever be a problem with a loss of the secret formula, any lab could take the liquid and break it down to its raw state. Then the formula could be recreated from that information.

Minute by minute and hour by hour, our attorney asked more and more questions meant to reveal the fact that David Townsend ran an elaborate scam, milking his company of resources from his home. Glickman challenged every past statement Townsend had made to show them to be either lies or contradictory to his new comments.

Townsend claimed on the stand that executive committee meetings were seldom held at his house. "Only those I had a real deep interest in, and then we would sit down and have a meeting. There were a lot of executive meetings also held at the office, too. He said that there was a big board room for the purpose of executive board meetings, and he was always in attendance."

In the earlier deposition, Townsend had claimed that the board met every week, with the important meetings held once a month at his home. The minutes of the home meetings were kept in the "red book," the special corporate minute book whose maintenance is required by law. The other board meetings were not.

Glickman began reading into the record:

Q: Well, if Anafuel was in business about two years, does that mean that the important board meetings of Anafuel were at the house?

A: All except the first one. After that a number of meetings were held at the house.

David Glickman, having read that section of the deposition into the record, asked: "Was that correct information that you gave at the deposition?"

"No," admitted David Townsend. Then he went on to say:

"I don't know why I said that. I know you got the deposition. You got it there. If I were reading it to myself, I would think to myself, I lost my mind, because we didn't hold all the board meetings at the house."

"Well, you were in good health when you gave that deposition," commented Glickman.

"I thought I was."

Our attorney then asked, "Were you sick when you gave your deposition?"

And Townsend replied, "I think so. I really don't recall that part of the deposition at all."

After hearing the endlessly changing stories by the extremely uncomfortable David Townsend, Judge Letteau facetiously asked, "Why are we reading all this testimony? Just to show that there are enormous discrepancies and contradictions between the live testimony and his deposition?"

"No," said Glickman. "I think that has been demonstrated already."

The judge, with what sounded like a smile in his voice, remarked, "Absolutely."

The testimony continued. There were questions about the sale of rights to distribute Anafuel, questions about the distribution of corporate funds, and other issues. The shooting was no longer of primary interest in the courts. That was an accepted fact. The question was liability.

By the time David Townsend, still dressed in his orange jail jumpsuit, finished testifying, the constant changes in story disgusted the judge. It was obvious that Townsend was lying. The only question was where and when he might actually have been telling the truth. Before he left, Judge Letteau said:

"How can you believe anything Mr. Townsend testified to? How can this court believe anything he testified to? He never says the same thing twice. I don't know if he's telling the truth now and lied in his deposition repeatedly, or if he's lying now and he told the truth in his deposition. How would I know?"

◆ ◆ ◆

David Crockett was the next person to testify under oath. As both a director and the secretary/treasurer of Anafuel, he said he was able to learn many of the "dirty little secrets" of what was taking place in the Townsend home office. Crockett was also one of the victims. The Texas indictment of David Townsend for which he had been arrested in the courtroom involved the forgery of Crockett's name on Anafuel checks. Townsend was using the checks in order to make personal purchases, but they needed a second signature which Crockett would not have given. The forgeries were meant to get around requirements of the corporation. Even worse, the checks, which totaled approximately nineteen thousand dollars, were written on closed Anafuel accounts.

According to further testimony, not only had David Townsend written checks for his family's groceries using the corporate account, but there were also credit card problems.

"I personally guaranteed, when I applied for corporate American Express credit cards for Anafuel, I guaranteed American Express, when it looked like the business was going to get going, because I knew we would need those things. There was never one dollar paid towards those accounts. The Townsends and the family used them religiously just as fast as they could, as soon as they got them in their hands."

The charges were for "everything from permanents to pantyhose to car tires, rent on their apartments and homes. And the bill befell on me for . . . fifteen, twenty thousand dollars."

One of the first areas of discussion was the success of the additive. According to Crockett's testimony, "Before you can come up with the finished gasoline ready for use in an automobile, you must first manufacture the additive. That is manufactured in small quantities inasmuch as it is co-blended or commingled with alcohol. And then the alcohol is commingled and blended with your petroleum-based product, which makes final finished product of gasoline."

"So the additive which was the secret proprietary formula, formulation, product, is made in small quantities." Unfortunately for the company, it also never sold. "There was contamination of the fuel mixture so the finished gasoline could not be sold. The gasoline turned black, and the color alone made it unsalable."

Crockett related that Townsend went into business with a group of Texas businessmen, selling them the patent to the primary formulation for the gasoline created from his additive. However, the patent had already been assigned to Anafuel and could not be transferred without board approval, which he did not have.

The patent was also sold to Petrolife, another Townsend company created in Texas. In addition, he used Anafuel money to buy a house in Houston, placing the house in his own name.

As Crockett went on, his own angry feelings heightened. "It is my opinion that Mr. Townsend has no respect whatsoever for the law, totally without integrity. He's a vile man."

Judge Letteau, who had been listening closely to the testimony, said, his tongue firmly in cheek, "Those are the good things you have to say about Mr. Townsend. Do you have anything critical to say?"

The story that continued to unfold seemed to spell out failure. The office records that were not in the Townsend home had been in a rented office near the mixing facility. Anafuel was evicted from the office in the fall of 1985, and the directors had to physically remove everything, dividing whatever would not fit in the Townsend residence among the homes of the various directors.

There was another eviction from the Texas offices, again for non-payment of rent. The utilities had been shut off, as had the telephone.

As other witnesses were called, their testimony seemed to indicate that David Townsend was offering some of the directors stock in exchange for future work. Although the arrangement was agreeable, it was illegal under California law. That fact was not known to the employees, though the assumption was made that David Townsend should have been aware of the law when he made such offers.

The vice president of marketing Raymond Arsnow's

testimony raised one important point concerning David Townsend's operations that had not been discussed earlier. He made it clear that it was known that Anafuel's product did not work in large quantities before the company began expanding into Texas, seeking investors for the same patent process.

The additive did work in small quantities, though, and Arsnow was made a believer when he used it in his own car. He stated, "The basis of the problem is that you heard of the ethanol mixtures of alcohol. The ethanol stories are in the paper with some regularity. The problem with it, when you get 10 percent ethanol or methanol, for that gasoline, the minute you put it into the beaker of a mixture you get what is called a phase separation. The alcohol separates immediately from the gasoline.

"In that position what would happen, you are driving down the road or you drive in and get some gasoline that has the allowable limit—which I remember has properties of at least 2 percent in your local gas station—and you pour that into your gasoline tank with a methanol gasoline mixture, you instantly have a phase separation. So therefore, what you are putting into your carburetor is straight methanol and your car doesn't run at all—well, unless it's very hot and you are going seventy, eighty miles an hour. Okay. Then it will run very well. Or if you are tuned to that effect.

"The basis of Anafuel or the process, and very little of this worked, and because I took the gasoline I made in the laboratory and put it in my car and it worked, you could take a 40 percent mixture of methanol and add that, which is the basis of Anafuel, and put it in 10 percent water and it would all stay together.

"You could take it or you could put it in a vibrator—what is the word I am looking for, those things you clean things with—in other words, you could shake the mixture by any means you could work out. I've frozen it in my freezer at home. I did everything I could to phase separate it and I couldn't do it. It was absolutely in the laboratory a fantastic product.

"Now the basis of that is that in the event we could get to just 25 percent methanol in your gasoline, you will cut your emissions, your carbon emissions by 66 to 68 percent, and the other emissions by about 45 percent. Now, in the Los Angeles basin that would probably clear up the smog problem."

Unfortunately for David Townsend, the limit for production seemed to be ten gallons. Batches made in larger quantities failed to work. "There's got to be a long chain molecule, carbon molecule that holds it all together, and apparently when you make it in large quantities that molecule breaks down."

The next surprise came when John Cejka, a man with a doctorate in physics who worked as a consultant for David Townsend, testified. He explained that while David Townsend originally had the patent on the process used for the Anafuel product, he assigned it to a company called Union Tank Car at the time he was working for them. This was before Anafuel, and when he also assigned the patent to Anafuel, he was breaking the law.

◆ ◆ ◆

Witness after witness spoke. Mark and I felt each of them linked David Townsend with Anafuel. We felt there was no question that he used the corporation any way he wanted, without trying to make the company a success. "I think there is just enormous proof of bad faith here," our attorney, David Glickman, told the court. "I mean, talk about diversion of corporate assets. He sold stock, yet pocketed the money himself. That's a diversion of corporate assets. So people, investors, or stockholders apparently put some money in the corporation. He wrote checks out of the corporation for cars for his kids, cars for his daughter-in-law, household living expenses, Jeffrey's criminal defense. He stripped the corporation of all the assets. That's a diversion of corporate assets so that there's nothing left to levy upon except the insurance policy, which is an asset."

Our attorney pointed out that it was the insurance company that would have to pay based on winning an independent action against a defendant, even when that person is insolvent. Because Townsend and Anafuel were one—the "alter ego" aspect of the case—the insurance company would have to pay for the negligence. More important, the Townsends' negligence was the same as negligence by the corporation, for which the insurance company was liable.

"I'm not sure young Jeffrey could have the requisite intent at age twelve with horseplay to be found guilty of an intentional tort. Kids horseplay all the time," our attorney firmly stated. "And adults may be held to a higher standard than a person age twelve.

"And I think this is a conscious sequence of events by David Townsend and Anafuel." Glickman's voice was steel-edged now. "He just used it to rip people off, and that is the difference here. I think the court said early this morning, it's a two-edged sword, putting the house in the corporate name by recorded deed—a fraud—but the entire corporation is a fraud, and the entire corporation is David Townsend. We're really talking one, the same conduct here, and I think that's where alter ego applies. I think David Townsend's abilities are equal to the corporation's agents and the liabilities are the same."

In closing, David Glickman quoted other cases that had established the case law. He then put into evidence the relevant documents from the testimony of the various individuals involved with the case. Finally, it was time for the judge to decide our case.

Chapter XXI

A VICTORY OF SORTS

On Friday, March 2, 1990, feeling apprehensive and nervous, we were seated in the courthouse at 9:00 A.M. Whatever the judge's decision, our lives would never again be the same. If the judge ruled against our lawyer, the insurance company would pay Dwayne little or nothing. If he ruled in our favor, then the carrier, a company called National Union, would have to pay. If the money involved was great enough, Dwayne would be able to have the long-term care he so desperately needed. The money would assure physical therapy, new medication when appropriate, and access to mechanical and electronic devices that could give him greater mobility. The future quality of Dwayne's life would be determined by the decision.

Judge Letteau seemed almost angry as he spoke. His words were objective, but it was obvious that he was deeply concerned about the actions David Townsend had taken. He did not address the possible liability of the insurance company at that time, but his conclusions were heartening.

"Based on the various witnesses who testified," the judge stated, "based on the abusive practices of Anafuel, it seems that the corporation itself—while it may have had a few real people and, arguably, some corporate objectives—was really a sham, and it was nothing more than David Townsend, his manipulation, his control of the entity itself and of the individuals employed by the entity. A terrible situation."

He continued, "We have also discussed the issue of negligence, and I think we all agree . . . that clearly the negligence in this case in the court's mind is in David Townsend and his wife allowing the gun to be left in a place where the young child, Jeffrey Townsend, could gain access to it. That's the negligence."

Then Judge Letteau commented, "Townsend was such a bad guy, he didn't care about anybody but himself. He certainly didn't care about Anafuel, just an incredible individual. I never believed that he had any concern about Anafuel. He was just concerned about bilking people out of their hard-earned money. I don't believe that Townsend was concerned with anybody but himself. I really don't."

We agreed with him. When it was over, we had won the first victory against the Townsends. In our hearts we knew that if he had been willing to show any compassion, we would not have been in court. And we felt that if he had not schemed so intensely to avoid paying, we would not have an insurance settlement that would enable us to give Dwayne a chance for a productive life.

What we did not know was that this was the beginning, not the end. Judge Letteau ruled that the Townsends and their corporation were liable for negligence when they left a loaded revolver unlocked and available to a minor. More important was the fact that was quoted in the *Los Angeles Times:* "Letteau ruled that the now defunct corporation was a 'shell company' and the 'alter ego of David Townsend,' clearing the way for the McKees to sue the corporation."

On March 24, 1990, the "final" settlement in the case came. Judge Robert Letteau considered several factors in assessing the penalty. The first was the fact that National Union, the insurance company, was not only liable but had avoided its responsibility by not even attempting to settle for any of the policies covering the house. This meant, among other things, that there would be economic damages, pain and suffering costs.

We had no idea what any of this could mean. All along, all we had sought was fairness and, ideally, a little compassion from those involved. Had a representative of National Union come to Mark and me at the very beginning, showing us the policies and offering to settle for the full amount, we would have been thrilled. The money would have been far less than Dwayne would need throughout his life, but there would have been fairness in all this. In fact, had the Townsends shown any compassion or concern whatsoever, their reaction coupled with a sum that would help cover the current medical bills would have satisfied us. We would have considered the situation as fair as possible under circumstances where true fairness could not exist.

Instead, everyone avoided responsibility. We were harassed. We were forced to face horrendous debts. We had to worry each day about Dwayne's future. Then we were faced with a year-long court battle during which Dwayne might have died.

All of this helped constitute pain and suffering, for which we discovered the insurance company could be held responsible. We did not know for how much until the judge ordered the company to pay Dwayne $8.5 million. The amount was based on a combination of the actual cost to keep Dwayne alive and as productive as possible through the next fifty years, as well as paying the lawyer and other costs. Although the sum sounded impressive, and it received headlines in several newspapers, in truth it was not. The horrifying reality of Dwayne's condition was that, invested wisely, Dwayne's share of the money probably would just meet the cost of future hospitalizations, medication, physical therapists, and special equipment to assure mobility. It would not set him up in an expensive house or provide him with elaborate entertainment facilities. He would still have to earn his own way, still be able to live only as nicely as his paycheck from whatever job he could hold would allow. The money solely meant that we could live with the knowledge that when we died, no matter what the circumstances of the rest of the family, Dwayne would probably not have to be institutionalized.

Another consolation was the fact that David Townsend had been led from the courtroom in handcuffs. His well-tailored clothing had been replaced with what looked like a glow-in-the-dark orange jail jumpsuit. Ironically, it was the same type of garment his son had worn to testify at the hospital. He had been humiliated, and for an alleged con man, losing his carefully constructed image can be almost as painful as losing money.

Nonetheless, what we had learned from the doctors during the trial about Dwayne's future was shattering. It was also compounded by what we now learned about the legal system. It is possible to be assaulted by procedures as brutally as by guns and bullets. Our lawyer, David Glickman, explained that National Union probably would not meet their court-imposed obligation without a fight that could last at least five years. Glickman would lead us through the battle, but like us he would not get paid until it was all resolved. We found that the harassment we endured from the deliberate actions of those who telephoned us, tried to terrorize Kimberly that night on the bridge, and all the other things that were done were minor compared with what National

Union might do. If National Union decided not to pay without a protracted fight, it meant that Dwayne might die before he was reimbursed for his suffering. And if that extreme horror did not occur, he might be faced with a life of far more disability than would be the case if we could afford the type of care needed for him.

I felt enormous pain and outrage when Dwayne was shot. Now I felt that we could be manipulated by corporate America, with no one claiming responsibility for the nightmare that was destroying my family's security.

As David Glickman had warned, in the next few months we learned the insurance company was going to fight. Appeal after appeal was launched, and each legal action, including the Supreme Court's decision, resulted in the same verdict—National Union was obligated to pay the judgment against them in this case. Finally, in September 1993, representatives of the company met with us and our attorney. At that time they made an offer to settle for what we later joked was "slightly less" than the $8.5 million judgment—$200,000. Such a settlement would have been a little more than 5 percent of the amount Dwayne would probably need to have adequate care over the next few years. We had no choice but to turn it down and insist that the insurance company meet the obligation determined in court. And so the wait continues.

Yet despite the aggravation, the financial problems, and the fears for the future, a few months after the joy of winning the court case and the emotional shock of discovering that the insurance company would appeal the decision, another incident occurred. It was an event for which our family had hoped and prayed, but never expected.

Chapter XXII

SMALL MIRACLES

The therapy session began like all the others. Willie carefully began rotating Dwayne's foot, stretching the muscles, manually duplicating an athlete's warming-up exercises. Then, as he had done so many times before, Willie prepared Dwayne to stand.

Leather gloves were placed on Dwayne's hands. He needed the leather to keep from slipping on the parallel bars. He could grip adequately with his right hand, but his left hand was permanently curled under and useless for gripping. The left hand was rested on the bar and would slip when Dwayne applied pressure if he did not have the added friction provided by the glove.

Then came the special braces Dwayne had been using. There was the AFO, the plastic device that protected Dwayne's ankle from being wrenched or broken when he fell. There was the Swedish knee cage, which kept Dwayne's leg turned in the correct direction. Otherwise, he might wrench his knee because he could not work it properly.

Dwayne's right leg had greatly strengthened. He felt it worked almost normally, but as I watched him move the leg, it was awkward, like the movements of a young child who can walk and run, though without grace or full control.

Dwayne worked his arms onto the parallel bars, then kneeled forward from the chair, finding his balance, pushing down with his muscles. The chair wheels were locked in place so the chair would not roll.

Dwayne began to sweat almost immediately. It was another positive sign. For a long time after the shooting Dwayne lost the ability to sweat. He would work intensely hard, he face reddening from the exertion, his muscles exhausted. Yet no moisture would appear on his face. Something about the severed nerves or some other part of the trauma caused by the bullet prevented him from sweating.

Now that had changed. His body lost moisture very quickly, cooling him during his exertions. His forehead, back, chest, and arms became slick from sweat. Without the gloves, he would have trouble maintaining balance and leverage on the bars.

As Dwayne rose to a standing position I could see the intense effort, his face contorted, sweat running down his cheeks. Willie gave him little encouragement because none was needed. Dwayne took pride in this accomplishment and had repeated it enough times to know that he could do it. What he did not know was that once he was upright, Willie had a further effort to ask of him.

Eventually Dwayne was erect. His wheelchair was behind him, the locked wheels acting as a backstop. If Dwayne fell backwards, the chair would cushion his fall. The force of such movement would knock the chair backwards, but the blow would hopefully be such that Dwayne would not break his neck.

That was the trouble with physical therapy. In order for Dwayne to progress, there was constant risk. It was one of the reasons I usually stayed to watch. It was also why I was glad that Willie had the strength, reflexes, and quality training to catch Dwayne if he fell.

Willie had a stool that looked like a high secretary's chair without back or arms. It was on wheels, and he sat on it now directly in front of Dwayne, rolling himself backwards as Dwayne moved. He could brace Dwayne from the front, move with Dwayne, or leap up and catch him if there was trouble. Between the locked wheelchair and Willie on the stool, Dwayne was not likely to get hurt.

Suddenly Willie said, "I want you to move your right foot, Dwayne. You are going to walk." I gasped, my fear rising. I knew he was afraid of falling, afraid of further injury. Yet Willie pressed, "Dwayne, you are going to walk?"

Dwayne knew that he had been working toward this moment, yet he really did not want to face it. What if it was hopeless? What if the little movement he had was lost because his balance was bad and he struck the floor too hard?

"Dwayne, *now*," Willie was insistent. I watched Dwayne straighten his body. Tired, Dwayne would let his left side sag, preventing himself from keeping effective control. Now he shifted himself so he was upright, the curvature kept to a minimum. Then he slowly, smoothly, lifted his right foot from the floor and moved it above the carpet several inches forward. The movement was normal, seemingly from the hip. The step was not so high or so long as it would have been prior to the shooting, but it might have passed for a casual stroll by someone with no place to go and in no hurry to get there.

Dwayne put down his right foot, then worked to catch his balance and to slow his heart following the exertion. He steadied himself again, careful to raise his left shoulder to keep from sagging to one side as he carefully raised his left foot.

The left side was the weaker side. He had to think two or

three seconds ahead of his action, raising the foot so that it at least skimmed the floor, then concentrating. Although the right leg had little trouble, the nerves damaged by the bullet sent his left leg into barely controllable spasms when he moved it. He worked the foot in increments, always moving it a little higher, a little further ahead, though without the smoothness of the right side. This time there seemed to be whole body action, less controlled by the hip as you or I would be.

Finally, Dwayne set the foot down. Perspiration poured down his face; his arms strained.

The right foot moved again, then the left. He worked to keep the foot straight, though his left foot and hip rotated inward a bit. He had to keep his shoulders back, had to work to keep the foot straight, had to fight the spasms.

Each time he paused, Dwayne tried to tell his therapist he could go no farther, but Willie would not hear of it. He was encouraging, insistent. Dwayne had learned to trust him, to meet the challenges Willie threw at him. Yet Dwayne lacked faith in his own abilities. He was afraid to be the way he was, afraid to fail in his efforts.

I knew how frightened Dwayne had become of life. He had been a fearless child, willing to try any activity. He frequently misjudged his abilities, falling and hurting himself, then trying again and again until he learned the necessary balance or gained the necessary strength. There was nothing he would not try; he was the type of athlete who succeeds regardless of innate ability, because he is willing to push himself beyond his present limitations.

The bullet destroyed all that. Dwayne learned in an instant that he was not in control of his own life. He could be brought down by the unexpected, shattered beyond repair. He had gained a fear of falling, of being in an automobile accident, of encountering Jeff Townsend or his brothers. Anything that might hurt him, anything from which he could not escape, led him into a world of fear he had never known existed before he was shot.

Dwayne was not a coward. He had great inner strength. But a part of his courage, a portion of healthy bravado, had been taken from him. He was aware of his vulnerability to others, his mortality, his inability to control even a portion of his own destiny. And because of that, it took a special trust to rise to Willie's challenge.

Inch by inch Dwayne moved closer to the end of the parallel bars where the bracing of the equipment would stop him. Altogether Willie wanted him to go no more than six to eight feet before turning around and walking back to where the chair was parked. It was a distance you or I would cover in seconds, far less time than it took Dwayne to cover each agonizing step.

The walk was not the kind of event that might be covered on one of the television sports shows. Had I been watching Mark deliberately pace himself so slowly, I would have fallen asleep. Some of Dwayne's moves were so limited that, had I not been staring at them, I would have missed them. Yet even the smallest distance meant remarkable progress.

Finally, after more than a half an hour, a time during which most people can comfortably walk approximately two miles, Dwayne completed his walk. There were tears in my eyes and a smile on my face so intense that the muscles later hurt from the strain. Our son had done the impossible! He had accomplished what all the doctors said would never happen—Dwayne had walked.

He had walked a distance equivalent to the narrow dimensions of a very small room, and it had taken him more than half an hour to accomplish that feat. What mattered to me, and I hoped to Dwayne, was that he had proven that he did have courage. His heart had not been shattered. He had discovered that despite the fears, despite the bitterness, the anger, and limitations, he could do the impossible.

That agonizingly slow, extraordinarily tiring walk did *not* mean he would one day run the streets of our community. It *did* mean that he could go to school, get an education, get a job, love a woman, share a life, and raise a family. His body was limited, but not his heart, his mind, or the essence of his existence. That walk showed me that Dwayne would live even if a physical portion of his body had died. He had found something deep within himself that he might never have discovered in a normal lifetime, and he had found that he could use it for his own benefit.

Jeff Townsend had told my son to say goodbye to life. The day he worked past all his fears, all his limitations, and did the impossible by walking, Dwayne McKee announced to the world that he was going to embrace life as he never had before. Dwayne had chosen to live, and the pride I feel for my son will be with me until the day I die.

Epilogue

A LIFE

The life of a quadriplegic is a delicate balance between hope and hopelessness. Dwayne took those first few steps with the help of the parallel bars, a feat he has repeated again and again, gradually strengthening his upper body and his legs but as yet never being able to go beyond that carefully braced distance.

To ensure that he doesn't backslide, Dwayne must walk at least twice a week with the help of his therapist, his braces, and the parallel bars. If he fails to do so, he needs intensive therapy for a week or more before he can be assured of standing for any length of time. The skills he constantly works to develop and maintain diminish when he misses even one therapy session. With progress there are always fears.

Quadriplegics are not like individuals with minor injuries in the way their bodies heal. If you or I break our legs or shatter our hips, ultimately we can walk with the use of crutches, canes, or some similar device. If a quadriplegic manages to one day use crutches, there can be deterioration of the shoulder. The sockets react abnormally compared with someone who is able-bodied though temporarily injured. Dwayne, walking on crutches, could erode the sockets, causing him to permanently lose the use of his arms.

Dwayne will always have to continue having therapy. He will spend the rest of his life working to maintain what mobility he has, and to increase that mobility to whatever degree is possible. Yet he is likely always to need a wheelchair, always to face the fact that meeting one physical challenge might mean that a previously mastered skill is lost.

Taking into account his physical limitations, Dwayne's future will be determined by his education, though even with a college degree there are hidden problems. The more he learns, the more that he can do—if someone is willing to look at his abilities and not his limitations, and if they can accepts his good and bad days.

As Dwayne's parents, we will never fully know peace of mind. The money, if the insurance company should ever pay it, will help ease Dwayne's burden. It will assure that he can live on his own, even if he has to be assisted either part of each day or part of each week. Yet his future will be determined by how well he is prepared to work with his mind, with the limited use of his hands, and with the possible bias of potential employers.

As of this writing, we continue to fight the insurance company. They have lost appeal after appeal, proving our right to the settlement. Yet Dwayne is not a human being but a business concern to them. I don't know if National Union simply wants us to feel that it can "win" by wearing us down, if they are hoping that Dwayne will die so they can settle for less, or if they like prolonging the payoff so they can use the money to make more profits. All I know is that we spend too much time in courts and in lawyers' offices for what has been declared our son's rightful compensation. He needs the money to assure a barely adequate quality of life, and the terms of the insurance policy were such that we are acting properly in our request that they meet their obligation.

David Townsend could not escape the law as skillfully as his insurance company attempts to do. He was eventually sent to prison for fraud. After his release on parole he was reutrned to prison for a parole violation. We do not wish him ill, yet there is something satisfying in knowing that the courts felt he must be responsible for his improper actions.

Both Dwayne and I live in fear of meeting Jeff again. Dwayne fears physical violence from Jeff or one of his friends, violence from which he can not protect himself. I am fearful of my reaction. Will I become frightened, mentally reliving the night Dwayne was shot? Will I become angry, verbally or physically attacking Jeff, trying to cause him as much pain as possible so he can have even the tiniest understanding of what Dwayne must endure? Or will I ignore him, recognizing that the past is over, the present requires strength, and the future is not for us to limit by foolish actions?

Yet there is some happiness in our lives. Certainly there is joy in what our son has accomplished since that fateful June day in 1985. However, there is also the endless, irreversible sadness. Each day as I look at the wheelchair, the special bed, the parallel bars, the pool lift, and the other equipment few people ever need in their lifetimes, I am reminded of a chilling reality of our lives.

Despite his hard-won progress, a formerly vibrant, athletic, and intelligent teenager has grown to manhood aware that he will never know the potential that was his to achieve before Jeffrey Townsend picked up an unlocked, loaded revolver and fired a single .38-caliber bullet through the neck of Dwayne McKee.

NOTES

Chapter 5

page 42 (" . . . sold it as gasoline."): Deposition of David Townsend taken by David Glickman, Esq., on Thursday, June 9, 1988, at 11:35 A.M. Deposition for the case of *Dwayne McKee, a minor, by and through Mark McKee, his guardian ad litem, Mark McKee, LaVonne McKee, Plaintiffs, v. David Townsend, Marilyn Townsend, Jeffrey Townsend, a minor, Anafuel, Smith and Wesson, and Does 1 through 45, inclusive, Defendants.* Superior Court of the State of California for the County of Los Angeles; case no. NWC 10436; pp. 12–13.

Chapter 8

page 58 (" . . . that was right."): Deposition of Marilyn Townsend taken September 8, 1987, for the case of *McKee v. Townsend,* p. 22.

page 58 ("... were best friends."): Ibid., p. 17.

page 59 ("... at that point."): Ibid., p. 27.

page 59 ("... away from him."): Deposition of Jeffrey Townsend taken September 8, 1987, for the case of *McKee v. Townsend,* p. 25.

page 59 ("... fire it off."): Ibid.

page 59 ("... of David Townsend."): Ibid.

pages 59–60 ("... onto the floor."): Deposition of David Townsend taken by David Glickman, Esq., on June 9, 1988, for the case of *McKee v. Townsend,* pp. 43–45.

Chapter 10

page 86 ("... looking for me."): Deposition of Charles David Crockett in the case of *McKee v. Townsend,* pp. 85–86.

pages 86–87 ("... 'can't touch the house.'"): Ibid., pp. 12–13.

page 88 ("... State of California."): Ibid., p. 40.

page 88 ("... a new company."): Ibid., p. 43.

pages 88–89 ("... 'this is your room.'"): Ibid., pp. 45–46.

page 89 ("... divulge to the IRS."): Ibid., pp. 55–56.

page 89 (... to make purchases.): Ibid., pp. 57–59.

Chapter 19

page 163 ("... sold it as gasoline."): Deposition of David Townsend taken by David Glickman, Esq., on June 9, 1988, for the case of *McKee v. Townsend,* pp.12–13.

page 163 ("... gasoline in California."): Ibid., p. 13.

page 164 ("... Juvenile Court in Sylmar."): Appeal from the Superior Court of Los Angeles County, Superior Court no. NWC 10436, reporters' transcript on appeal, Vol. 1, p. 35.

pages 164–65 (“ . . . was on it.”): Deposition of Nancy Jean Harris taken on January 18, 1989, pursuant to subpoena by lawyers for defendant Anafuel Corporation, p. 11.
pages 165–67 (“ . . . the pistol was.”): Deposition of Davis Townsend taken December 1, 1988, Vol. 2, pp. 139–43.
pages 167–68 (. . . board of directors.): Deposition of Charles David Crockett taken February 18, 1989, pp. 15–20.
page 169 (“ . . . its rent there.”): Appeal from the Superior Court of Los Angeles County, p. 62.
pages 172 (“ . . . going to be.”): Appeal from the Superior Court of Los Angeles County, Vol. 1, pp. 81–82.

Chapter 20

page 187 (“ . . . Everything.”): Appeal from the Superior Court of Los Angeles County, Vol. 1, pp. 196–207.
page 190 (“ . . . as possible tomorrow.”): Ibid., pp. 219–20.
page 192 (. . . at the house.): Ibid.
page 194 (“ . . . deposition at all.”): Ibid.
page 194 (“ . . . How would I know?”): Ibid., p. 313.
page 195 (“ . . . twenty thousand dollars.”): Appeal from the Superior Court of Los Angeles County, Vol. 2, p. 356.
page 195 (“ . . . in small quantities.”): Deposition of Charles David Crockett taken February 18, 1989, p. 77.
page 196 (. . . his own name.): Ibid.
page 196 (“ . . . critical to say?”): Appeal from the Superior Court of Los Angeles County, Vol. 2, p. 367.
page 196 (. . . as had the telephone.): Ibid., pp. 386–92.
pages 197–98 (“ . . . molecule breaks down.”): Ibid., p. 452.
page 198 (. . . breaking the law.): Ibid., p. 463.
pages 198–99 (“ . . . which is an asset.”): Appeal from the Superior Court of Los Angeles County, Vol. 3, p. 923.
page 199 (“ . . . are the same.”): Ibid., p. 925.